Carlo Ferraris

Carlo Ferraris

Design
Gabriele Nason

Editorial Coordination
Filomena Moscatelli

Copyediting
Charles Gute

Copywriting and Press Office
Silvia Palombi Arte&Mostre,
Milano

Sales Department
Antonia De Besi

US Office
Francesca Sorace

Cover
Portrait of Mother, 2000

This publication was supported by

Florence Lynch Gallery, New York

Allegheny Productions LLC, New York

Edizioni Charta srl
Milano
via della Moscova, 27 - 20121
Tel. +39-026598098/026598200
Fax +39-026598577
e-mail: edcharta@tin.it

Charta Books Ltd.
New York City
Tribeca Office
Tel. +1-313-406-8468
e-mail:
international@chartaartbooks.it
www.chartaartbooks.it

Balancing Act of Life:
Carlo Ferraris's Photographic Work

Sabine Russ
German Art Critic and
Freelance Curator based in New York

In a dark room a man is about to descend a narrow staircase. He appears to light his way by holding an ornate electric chandelier. The black-and-white photograph is titled *The Stroll*. As in all of Carlo Ferraris's works (his photographs and films as well as his early sculptures) the situation is carefully staged. Every detail and gesture matters as part of an enigmatic ensemble. The "strolling" man looks hesitantly yet intently down the steps while the chandelier illuminates his face, rather than the darkness ahead of him. Where is he going and what does he see? There is a hint of Dante in this sparse and eerie setting; the protagonist could be on the threshold to the underworld, perhaps a post-industrial purgatory, while casually holding up a remnant of bourgeois lifestyle or religious ceremony. However, it is typical for Ferraris that he provides no clues for an interpretation of the scene.

The subversive power of Ferraris's imagery lies in its ambiguity and incongruity. He creates visual conundrums with the material of the everyday — from domestic settings to common people involved in peculiar activities. While his staged scenes at first may look quite ordinary and innocuous, they soon reveal some odd or illogical detail, an aberration from the norm or an outright paradox. Peril and mishap are imminent and, occasionally, feigned death occurs as a result of mysterious physical or psychological force. Often reminiscent of film stills (and some photographs are indeed films stills), the scenes suggest a complex narrative, a fraught before and after to which no further clues are given. It is also noteworthy that Ferraris frequently offers vague or merely faint references to religion by employing certain symbols or by evoking dimensions beyond the visible and knowable.

Untitled, *Nidge*, and *Here Far Away* — a group of photographs printed directly from the negative — suggest an ethereal, otherworldly realm. Interestingly, the featured objects were specifically prepared for the purpose. Ferraris

had a priest's robe tailored in white, only to have it
appear in the expected color (black) in the positive print.
A black wedding dress was sewn to emerge in lucent,
intangible white and a dinner table for two was set in
colors opposite to the ones appearing in the picture. The
scenes have a hazy, ceremonial air while being strangely
unsettling — without bodies to fill the clothes and chairs
they evoke a ghostly hereafter.

The cryptic nature of Ferraris's imagery, its subliminal
quality and dreamlike spirit, bring his work into the
vicinity of Surrealism. René Magritte and his mystifying,
unknowable paintings come to mind, as do the surreal
and disturbing scenes staged by the Spanish filmmaker
Luis Buñuel. What Ferraris shares with the artists of this
influential movement is a strong belief in alternative ways
of perceiving and depicting reality as well as the freedom
to forego explanations. A deep distrust in the
preconceived, the norm, or a universally applicable order
pertains as much to Ferraris as it does to the Surrealists.

On the Beach, an uncanny and perplexing photograph,
appears like a product of the subconscious or as if the
scene was conceived in a dream. It shows a man (the
artist) hunched over in the sand while the beach is staring
back at him many-eyed, namely with Ferraris's own eyes.
Shards of mirrors were slid into the sand and meticulously
trained so that each of them reflects the artist's right eye.
The result is a potent and unsettling image — a Narcissus
under surveillance by his scattered, cyclopean self and a
witness to his own multi-angled perception. Eyes —
displaced, mutated, and multiplied — figure prominently
in compositions by Magritte, Buñuel, and Max Ernst. With
Ferraris (as with the Surrealists), a picture can observe
itself as much from within as it is observed from outside
by the viewer.

Seeing and not seeing; light and darkness; reflections,
traces, and shadows are recurring features in Ferraris's

work. Yet, in his world of the inexplicable everyday,
perception and orientation are not limited to the visual.
Often, Ferraris's characters are involved in a sort of tactile
"seeing" — with gestures of groping, outlining, targeting,
or balancing. A number of scenes have an air of small-
town circus acts or backyard hocus-pocus.

In *Before the Show*, a grown man sits on one of
twenty-one empty chairs surrounding a blooming cherry
tree. He is contemplating the upcoming challenge of
mounting a child's wooden swing while everyone (or no
one) will be watching. The scene suggests a precarious
acrobatic act; however, downfall is imminent because the
meager tree won't bear the weight of an adult swinger.
The image strikes a familiar chord in everyone who knows
stage fright and embarrassment while it reveals Ferraris's
particular brand of understated humor.

At the core of his pictorial riddles are life's small and
large trials; Ferraris evokes them with an almost childlike
naiveté and intuition. Resulting in parodies of bravado
and failure, he poses more or less silly challenges to
objects around the house (*My Pen Collection* or *Lobbia*) or
has his characters perform bogus balancing acts. *The
Stroll II* features a man walking a tightrope. On closer
inspection you realize that the acrobat is one-legged and
isn't fit for "strolling" that way. *Man in the Doorway*
shows a juggler with a stack of apples that is held in place
by the upper beam of the doorframe. *Untitled* (2006) has
a man "doing" the hula-hoop in front of a wall covered
with newspapers. It turns out that the hoop around his
waist consists of wooden clothes pins fastened to his
body. All these tricksters are presenting their acts with an
utter seriousness and concentration that insinuates a
profound or even symbolic meaning. As one scrambles
through one's mind, performing one's own loops of
thought in search of a possible interpretation, one might
end up with no more — and no less — than comic relief.

Feet and Shoes is a puzzling and hilarious photograph featuring nine male lower legs (four pairs sitting, one leg standing). It is immediately evident that there is something wrong with this picture, but only at second glance does one realizes that the men are each wearing one of their neighbor's shoes. These are not the recruits desired for fighting a war. These feet will surely fail the goose step, whether on purpose or not. But what makes this simple image so deeply touching is how it exposes human vulnerability and dependency. It exposes our propensity to fall short of common sense or of the rules we created for ourselves. The challenge can be as basic as putting on shoes in a certain way or as difficult as respecting another dress code or belief system.

There is a refreshing genuineness and whimsy to Ferraris's approach that opposes the kind of cerebral efforts that are often necessary for "reading" contemporary art, frequently at the cost of immediacy and visual appeal. Rather than following current artistic trends, Ferraris relies on his own idiosyncratic vision. While he tackles somber themes such as impairment, disease, violence, and death, he does so in a slapstick and slyly manipulative manner. Playing with the viewer's associations and trains of thought, he subtly evokes stereotypes and metaphors only to twist them around or to dispose of them altogether.

In *Saturday Night* things have gone awry around a shabby sofa and a TV monitor on an equally shabby table. Strewn about are a pair of old-fashioned high heels, a blouse, a book, a cordless phone, and about two dozen red apples, each tossed after a couple of bites. Today's Garden of Eden is a cheap and lonely place with a TV screen retired to blank after a night's work of temptation. As the apples testify, the original sin took place excessively and wastefully. No traces reveal where God sent Eve for punishment (probably to bed).

Ferraris hints at faith and Christian iconography in a number of other works. For *Man and Baby*, father and son are posing like a *Madonna col bambino*, except that both have their heads covered with hoods, which leave only their eyes visible. Allusions to sainthood and terrorism are coupled in a brazen and farcical way. However, knowing that Ferraris's son was born the day before September 11, 2001, this work assumes a poignant personal dimension.

Although his imagery does not convey information about his private life beyond basic human experience, Ferraris is certainly motivated by his personal legacy. Priest and Madonna as well as references to Hell and Paradise attest to his Catholic upbringing. Luis Buñuel once famously remarked: "I am, thank God, an atheist." This kind of oxymoron also emerges in Ferraris's vision as he insidiously distorts and comically undermines symbols of faith.

Ferraris draws as much from his small-town background as he does from big-city life. In fact, he frequently returns from New York to his hometown in Northern Italy for inspiration as well as for locale and characters. A number of staged situations involve his elderly parents, his siblings, and his friends there, and several curious actions haven taken place around his family house.

For *Untitled* (1997), a skinny plum tree in his parents' garden underwent an unwarranted hands-on treatment. Acting like nature's accountant, Ferraris painstakingly numbered the leaves from one to more than a thousand (one can make out "1253" in the upper branches). The humble suburban tree became not only an eccentric monument to logic and efficiency, but also an homage to Arte Povera — to a movement of great experimental spirit and one that considered all parts of the human environment worthy of artistic intervention.

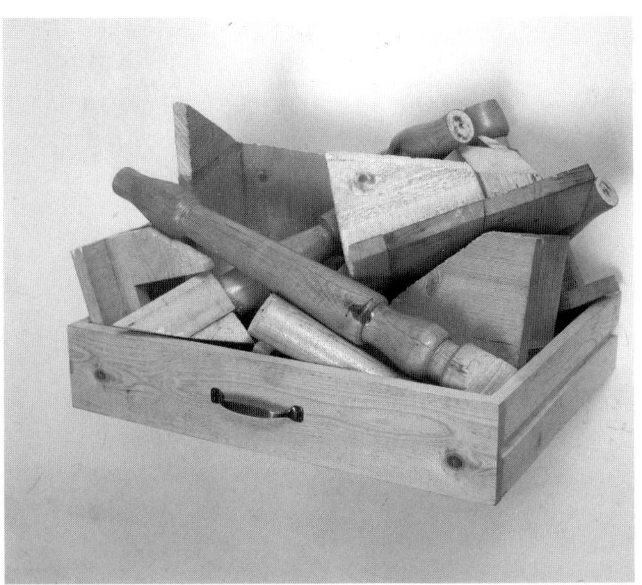

Table, 1993

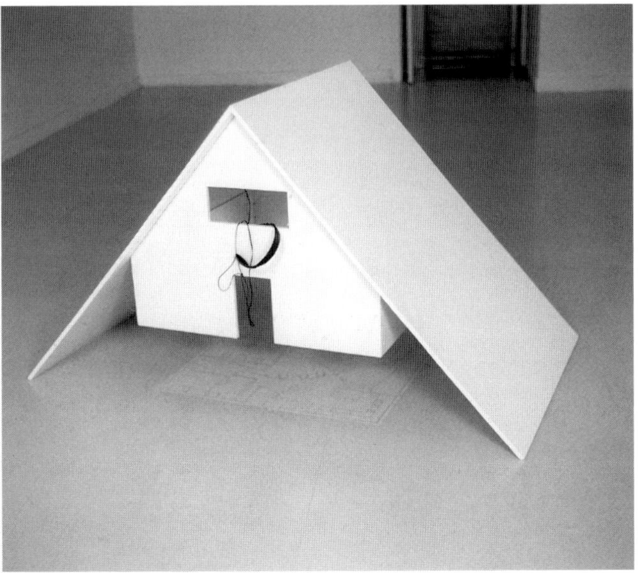

House, 2001

As with the numbered tree, Ferraris often engages in laborious and seemingly nonsensical efforts for the sake of producing a single photographic image. For a baffling photograph, simply titled *Blue Car*, Ferraris drilled by hand thousands of individual holes into the car's metal frame. The first association triggered by the pierced vehicle is that it came under fierce machine-gun fire. But depicted in a neutral surrounding landscape with the car's windows perfectly intact, this notion must quickly be abandoned. Again, things don't add up in a logical way. While war images inevitably cross the viewer's mind, in the end *Blue Car* remains a blue car with holes, an abused object, and as such it is both symbol and charade.

Another victim of Ferraris's intrusions on everyday objects is a dark-wooded set of living-room furniture including a television monitor, a lamp, and a few decorative items. All surfaces are speckled with small squares of pink tape, as if patched for blemishes. The formerly immaculate room looks as if befallen by a skin disease — a scarred chamber, quarantined from the rest of the house. By subjecting something as mundane and intimate as a private living room to ostensibly alarming, even epidemic conditions, Ferraris brings the outside world inside. While every child must believe in the safety and uniqueness of its home, inevitably there comes a moment of awakening: there is no such haven. Even the remotest and most isolated place won't be shielded from but instead will be afflicted by the larger forces and scourges of life. Wherever living occurs there will be stains.

The ill-omened domestic is a theme that has occupied Ferraris from the start. In this context it is important to consider his early sculptures, among them a table serving up its own cut-off feet and a chair with one of its legs extending into a lower story. A small model house was equipped with an audio spy system, which, when

9

activated by a motion sensor, revealed curious happenings in each room. Ferraris's approach to photography is still that of a sculptor, and he goes to remarkable lengths in producing the settings for his scenes. Many of his current works are preceded by, or based on, sculptural installations. His decision to present them in print rather than as physical objects might be due to his increasing involvement with producing films. Photography certainly suggests an additional narrative dimension to Ferraris's sculptural situations, even if an explicit plot remains at large.

If Ferraris's flawed objects defy purpose and function, his characters and their actions defy common sense. For a series of works devoted to the theme of death, Ferraris employed family and friends to act out pseudo-crime scenes. In *Falling Man*, a sequence of images featuring Ferraris's parents and siblings, a mock-homicide is staged. As if rehearsing for a home version of *The Godfather*, young and old are amateurishly pointing guns at each other. Family portraits have never looked like that. *Sons of the Surrounding Land* shows the outline of a victim around a cemented pillar of a building while onlookers seem to ponder the remarkable stabbing. *Woman on Sidewalk*, presented like a police photograph, features another unlikely fatal position. With the contents of her purse spilled on the ground, the woman has collapsed into a kind of yoga stretch that would be impossible to assume in case of sudden murder. Turning violence into parody and evidence into farce, Ferraris makes the bleak subject of death emerge as an admittedly bad joke. These works — along with others hinting at terrorism, industrial drama, and environmental hazard — confirm Ferraris's attention to pertinent matters of today. He is not out there to provide explanations or answers to the world's ethical and other shortcomings, but then, who can?

Surrealism evolved in the 1920s in response to World War One, a war that brought (with the first-time use of aviation) a new and universal dimension to military conflict, wrecking large-scale disaster on mankind both physically and psychologically. The new millennium, plagued by infinite tribulations, old and new, has propelled the world into an even less predictable and even more perilous condition: suicide bombings, epidemics, and ecological breakdown are a few of the latest threats to life. As we are all trying to make sense of this new era, it is not surprising that artists respond with a vocabulary of the surreal, the illogical, and the absurd. In fact, it is surprising that one doesn't find more artworks that share Ferraris's approach. Evoking the stuff that all children (young and old) are afraid of — impairment, failure, darkness, abandon, nightmares, illness, violence, and death — Ferraris nevertheless leaves us with powerful and persuasive images, the wit of which can be cathartic and the heart of which is deeply humane.

This book frames Ferraris's unique and impressive photographic oeuvre of the last fifteen years in a telling manner. It opens with *Untitled* (1993) (one of his earliest photographs), which shows the artist holding a large target disk in front of his upper body. The book ends with *Full Tunnel* (a recent work), featuring a middle-aged man lying flat on a patch of grass with his right arm groping and fully immersed in the ground. One protagonist being passive, the other active, both seem eager to receive or find something fundamental. Presumably, in the first case it is the clue to death while in the second it is the clue to life. But it is equally imaginable — and desirable — that each will receive both.

Carlo Ferraris
Double Meditations: The Video Works

Horace Brockington
Curator/Art Historian,
City University of New York, New York

In his videos Carlo Ferraris reinterprets his sculptural and photographic works so that two worlds co-exist by means of interference, reversibility and experimentation. Similarly in his films, the ordinary world and the objects that make it up become the points of experience, affecting our senses and understanding in new and unexpected ways. Narrative content is loaded with ambiguous irony. Often disjunction and opposition denounce a precise reading of situations while adding a strange depth to the unfolding occurrences.

Ferraris often subverts a formalist cinematic order; constant shifts in cinematic narrative structure confuse thematic intent. His cinematic nuances use a series of precise framings (close/far), focusing techniques (clear/blurred), and contrasting movements (jumpy/static). Typically no clear narrative is presented. As a result, stylistic devices in Ferraris's videos present various levels of reality. Ultimately the work is about the interface between cognition and consciousness, perception and mind. Nowhere is that more evident than in *Eastern Standard Time*, a narrative short film.

Eastern Standard Time is both a humorous and disturbing work. The narrative, with its deep Oedipal undertones, is about a young man's mental breakdown. Ferraris creates a world whose structure can at best be described as very counterfactual. The intermixing of segments has a pacing that is often found in music videos. In the middle of the video there is a self-promotional piece for the central storyline. As quickly as the viewer thinks they have discovered a definable narrative or formal structure to the work, *Eastern Standard Time* denies all rationale.

In one of the scenes a young man with a rotating symbol on his forehead is incapable of distinguishing between the words "pork" and "Porsche." We watch his decline as he gradually loses all comprehension of the real

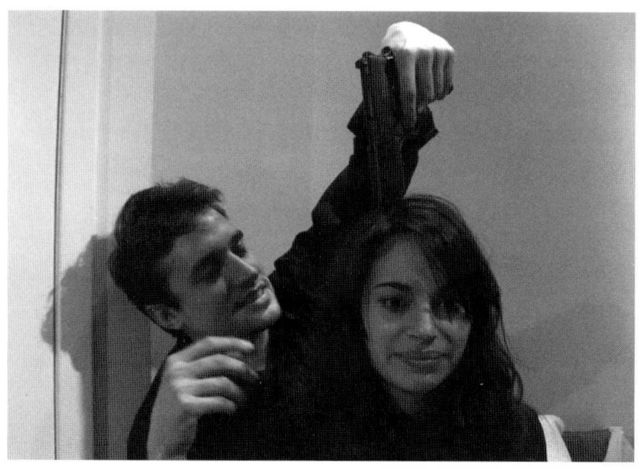

Still from *Eastern Standard Time*, 2005

world. These early symptoms develop in the beginning of the film when as a boy he accidentally shoots his father — a soldier in the Army — with his father's own gun.

Robert Rose described the central scene as patricide, though it must be understood as one loaded with comic potential. There is a humorous aspect to the manner in which Ferraris staged the ascension of the father's spirit through the bullet hole in the ceiling. The viewer is later presented with an ironic scene of the boy contemplating the mystery of his father's death as he peers through the bullet's entry hole in the rear of his father's combat pants. The final image of *Eastern Standard Time* reveals a damaged young man being observed by an interpreter as he struggles, with the help of a nurse, to salute nothing at all.

In *Eastern Standard Time*, Ferraris wants us to reflect on the situation of loss, while pointing out the absurdity of our adopted views of the world. By extension, the work shows us the traces left by war and tyranny. Incorporated into the video is a direct link with issues of violence and the nature of power (military/nationalistic). This echoes Walter Benjamin's concept of abuses of power in demographic regimes, as well as Foucault's concept of biopower and its consequences.

Similar to *Eastern Standard Time*, Ferraris's most recent work, a short 24-minute film titled *Osamu*, continues the play between the real and surreal. It is the story of a young man who from early childhood has fallen into an introverted depression. The film depicts conflicting stories of Osamu, who became isolated as a result of childhood trauma. Contextually, the film can be described as a story of a lonely man who is gradually losing contact with the world and alternatively creating a new reality through his imagination. However, we are never certain if this character is real or imagined. Overlapping narratives in this disjointed film — a characteristic element in Ferraris's

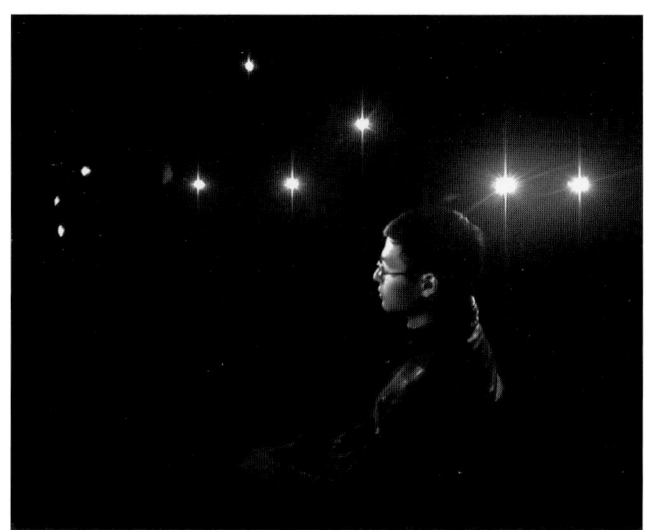

Still from *Osamu*, 2007

work — transform the film into a form of cinéma vérité. It is both an engrossing and disquieting work. *Osamu* is abstract while squarely based in a narrative context that is held together by the theme of surveillance and power. Characteristic of the artist's approach, the work is loaded with issues relating to abuse and inflicted violence.

As several vignettes evolve throughout the film, characters appear and reappear as if linked by a psychological construct that is never revealed. The actors, whose actions function as metaphors for the human condition, need to continuously navigate through ever-changing and often stressful realities that lead to an inevitably tragic conclusion.

In both videos violence and suffering is revealed as part of the human condition. The site of suffering is a place wherein emotions and wounds come together. As such, the work treats violence symbolically and allows for its working-through. Chantal Pontbriand has proposed that to see a suffering body is violence in and of itself. However, the violence is never overwhelming in Ferraris's works because it is softened by a lighthearted sense of humor.

Formally and conceptually, Ferraris's videos forge dialogues between points of opposition. They become vehicles for critiquing social and political issues. His art embraces issues of symbol and myth, presence and authenticity, the contradictory abuses of consumerism, and the promise of utopia. His art is explicitly reflective of the artist's curious bewilderment about humanity's position.

In general, Ferraris strives to establish a discourse in which the aesthetic reveals a reality that might provoke a moment of contemplation or displaced sentimentality. Through radical cinematic discourses he aims to involve the viewer into a type of emotional participation as a condition of the aesthetic experience.

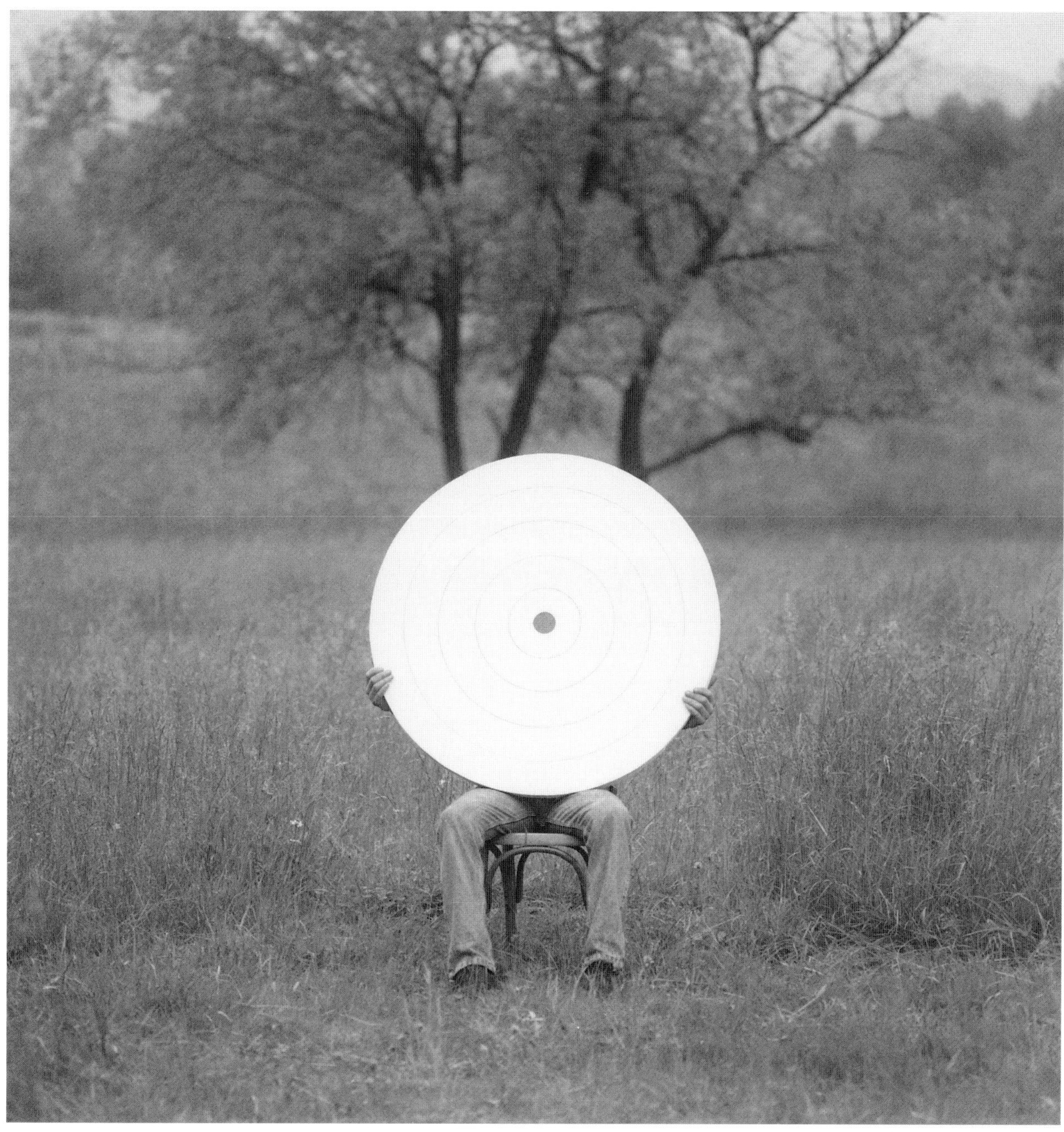

Untitled, 1993

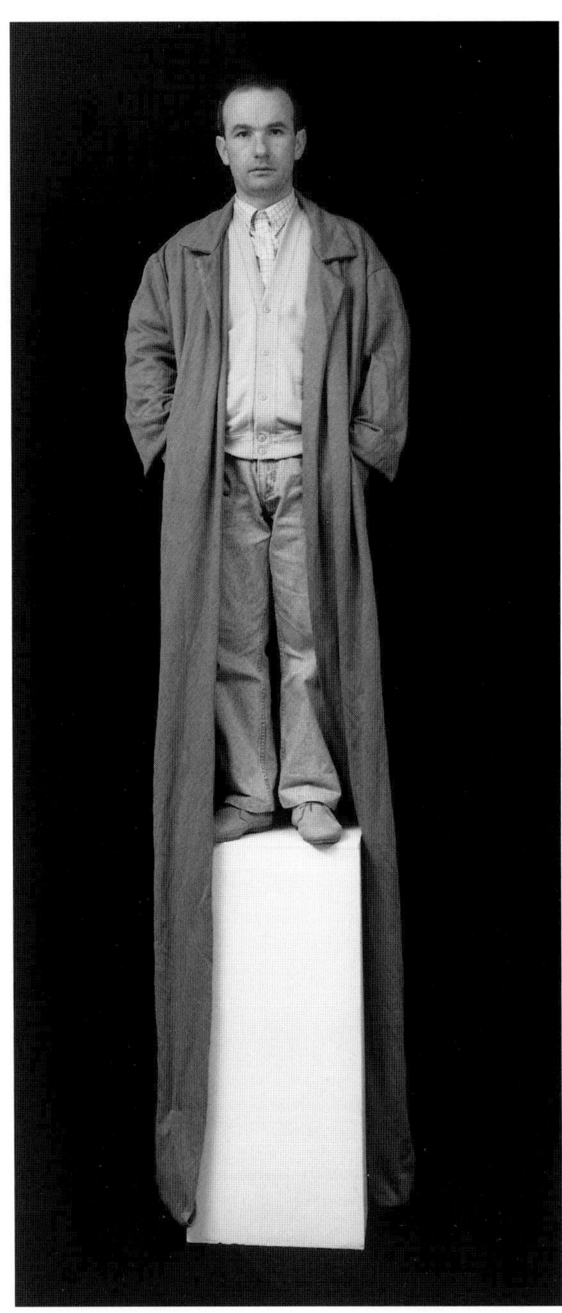

16

The Ambassador Has Arrived, 1994

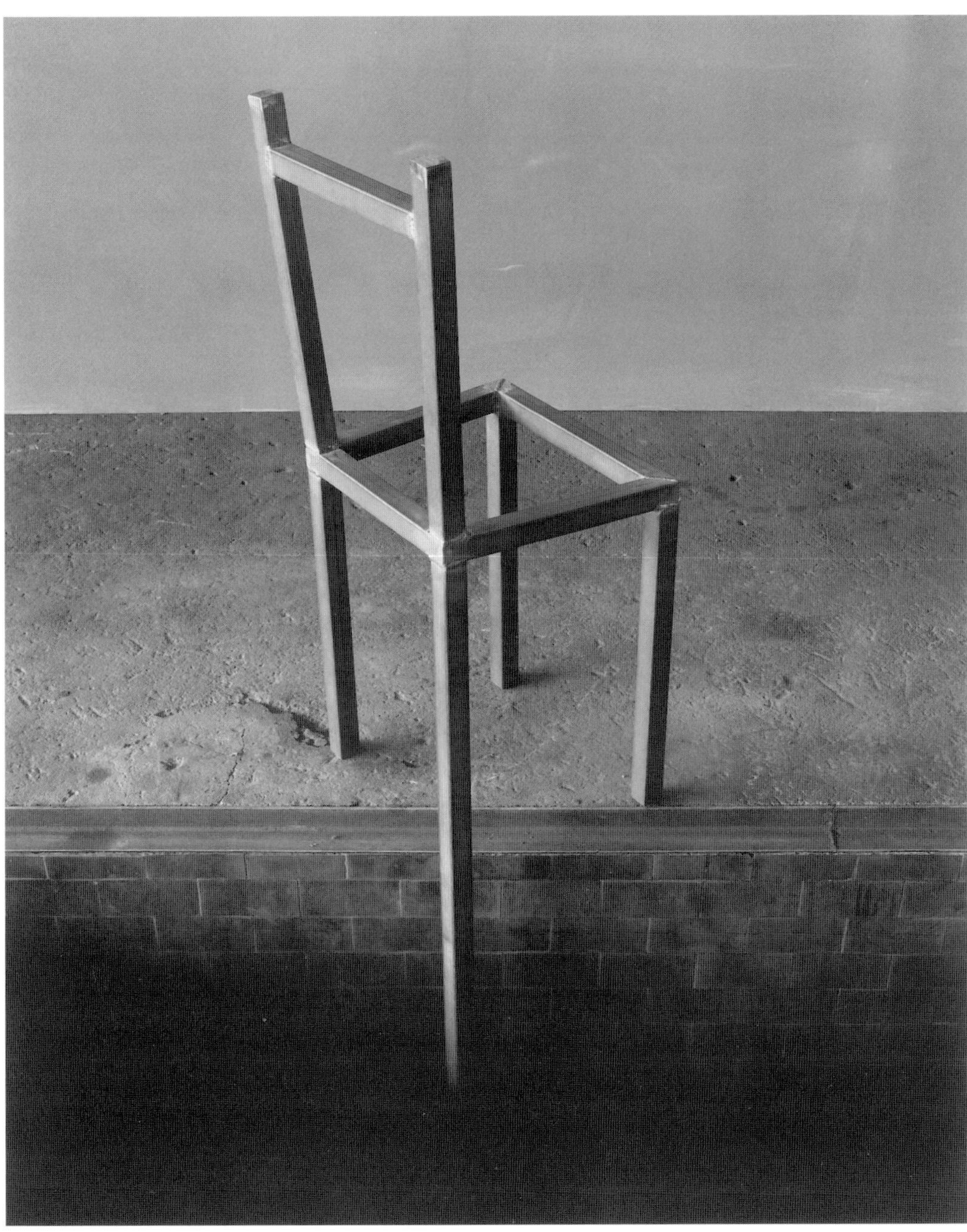

Requiem, 1994

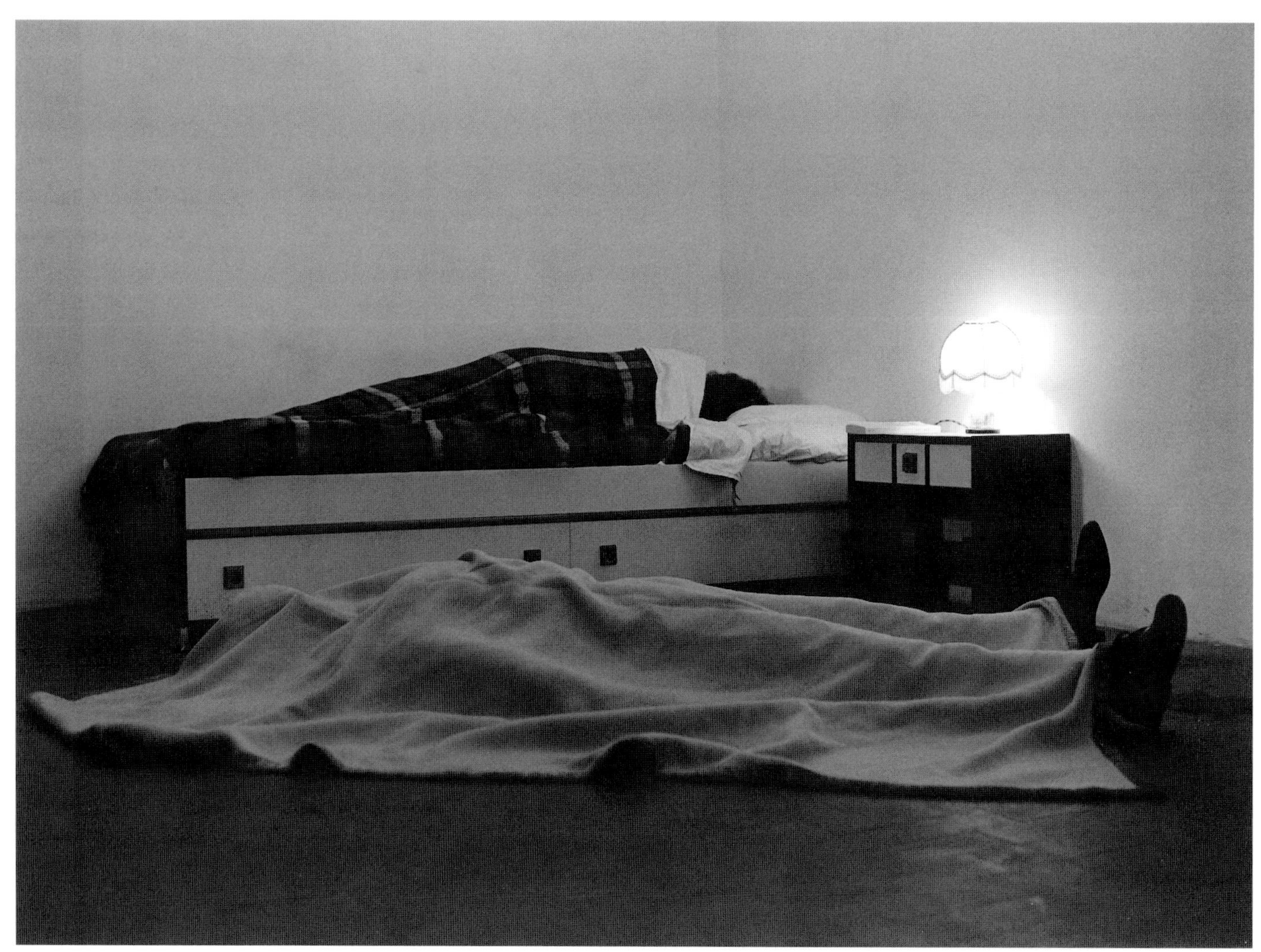

Oh if only I was born straighter!, 1994

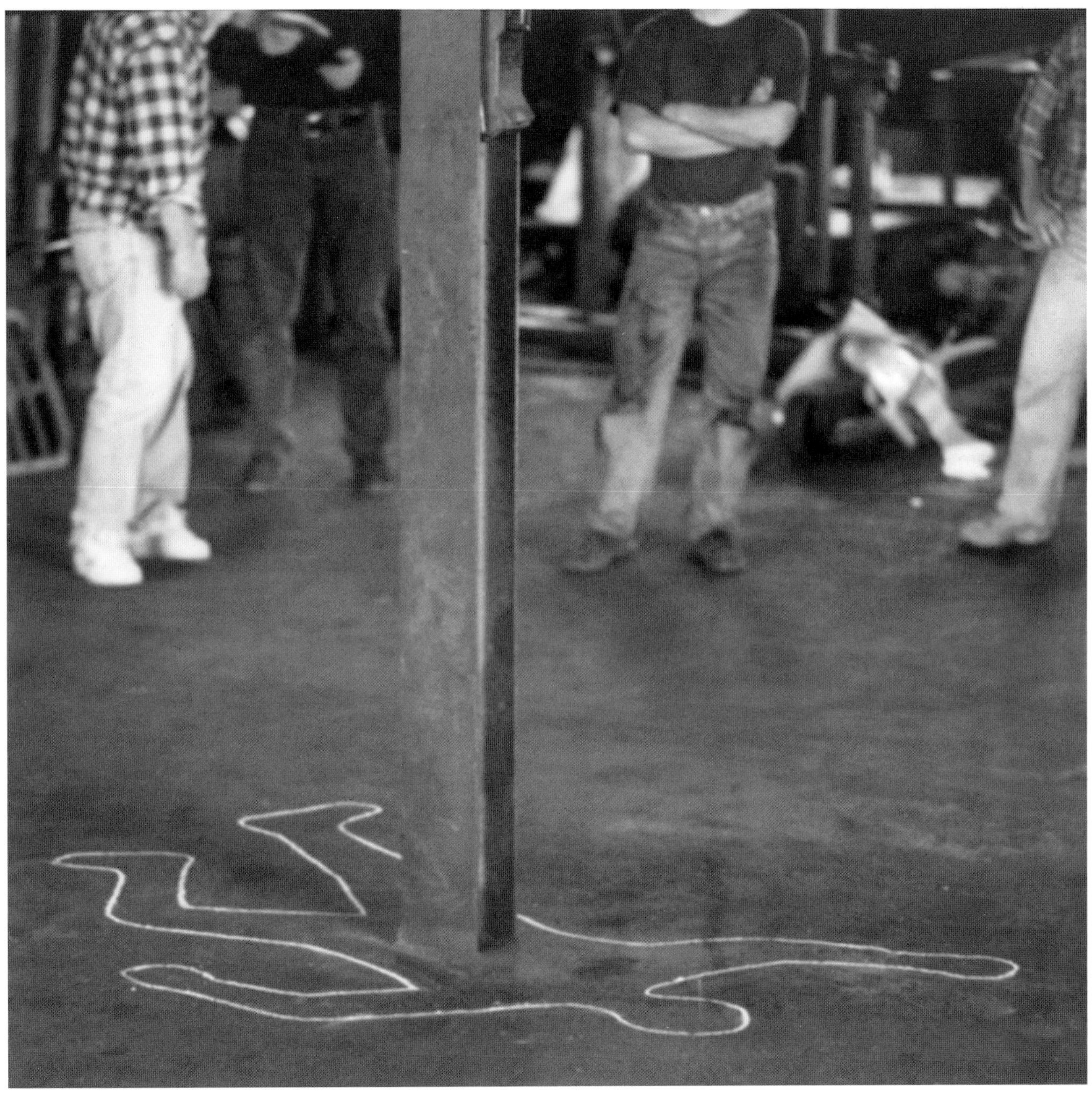

Sons of the Surrounding Land, 1994

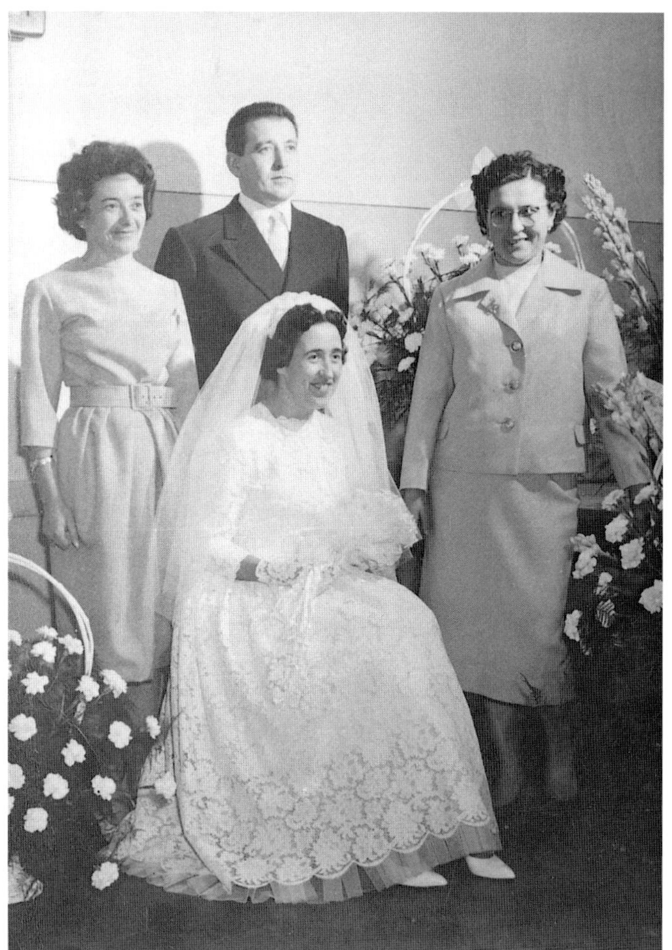 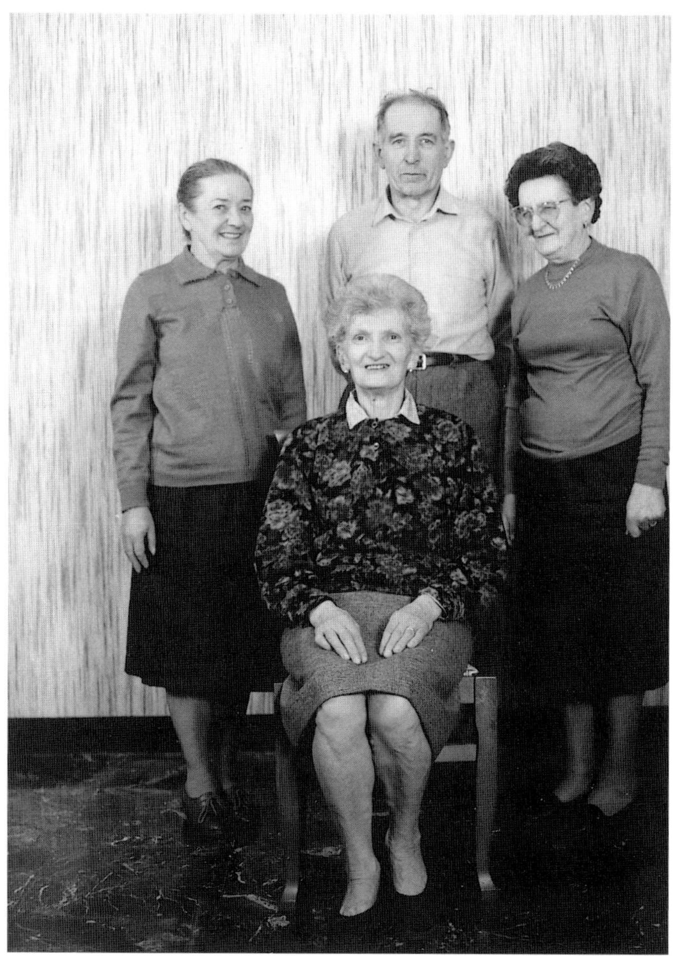

The Appointment, 1994

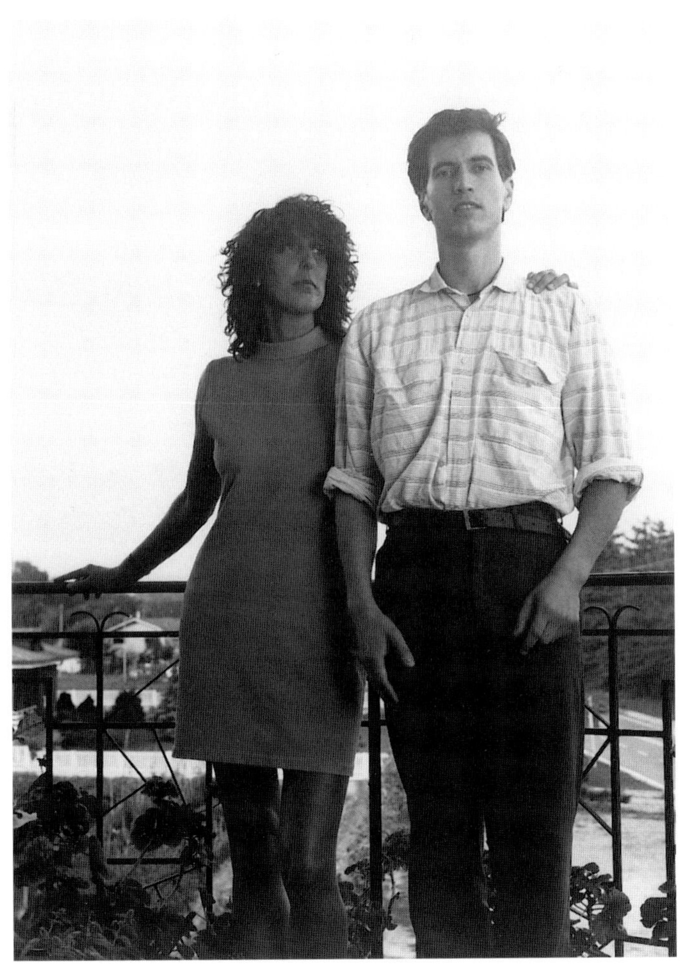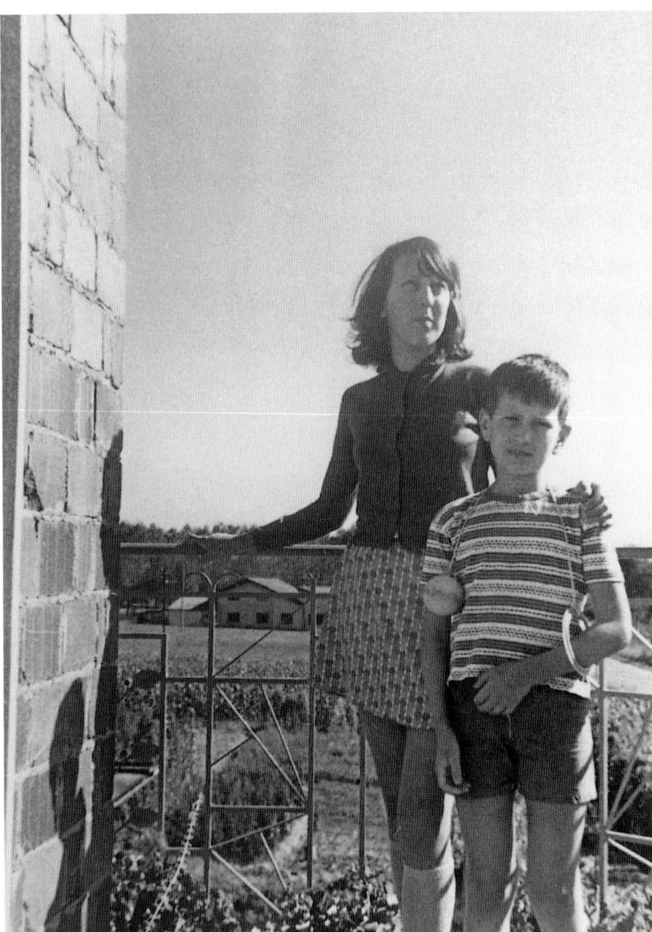

Self-Portrait with Sister, 1996

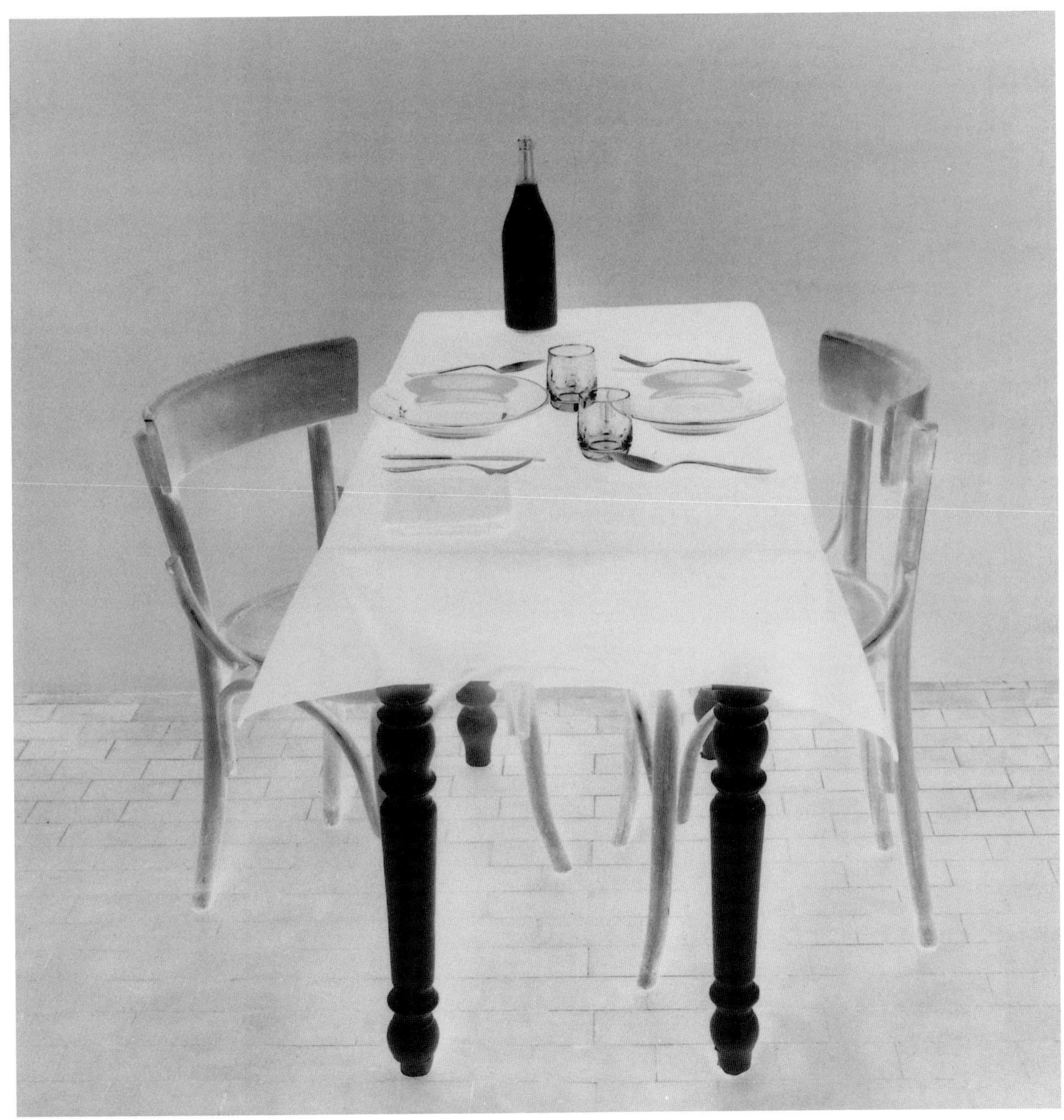

Here Far Away, 1994

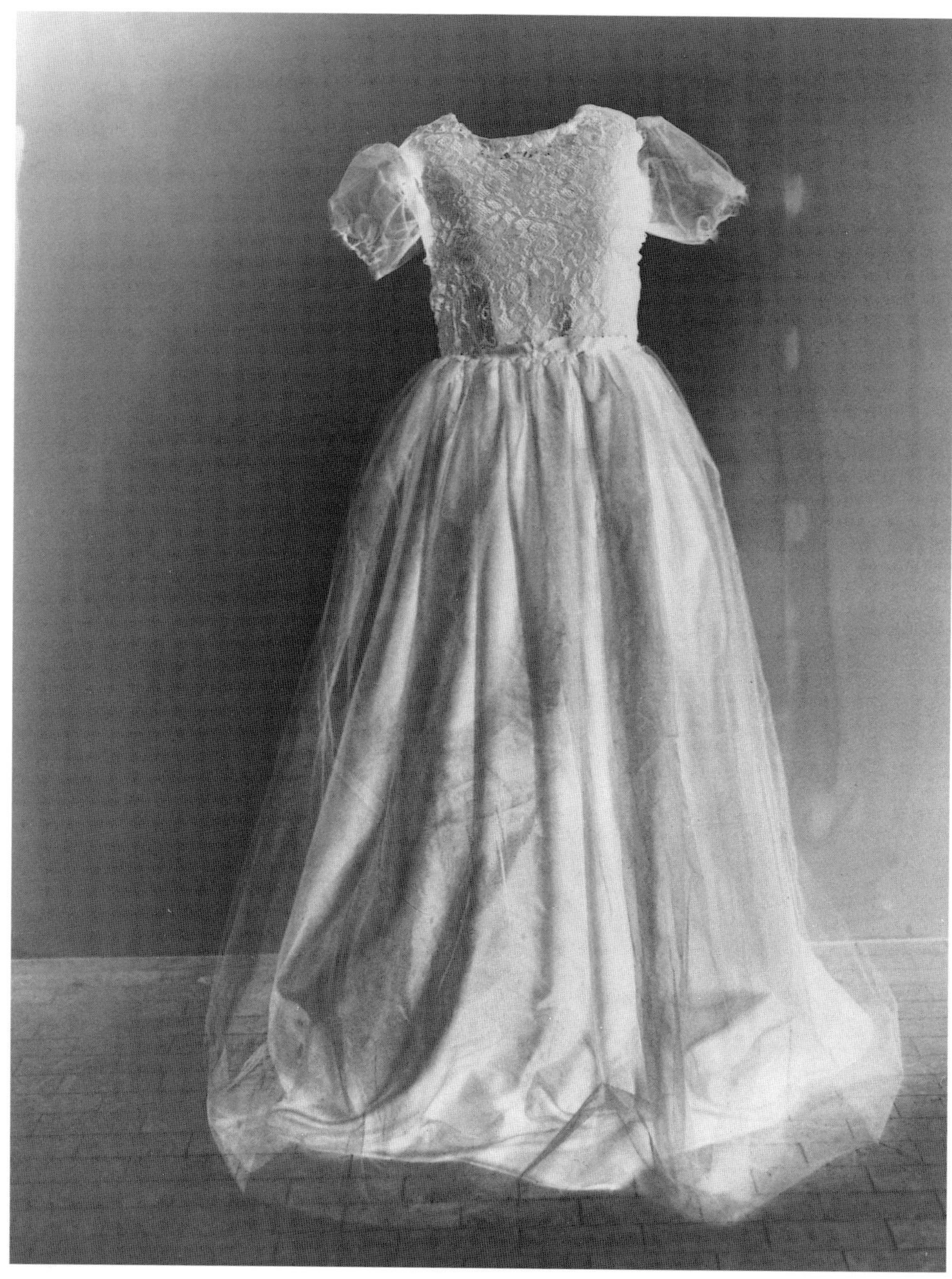

Nidge, 1994

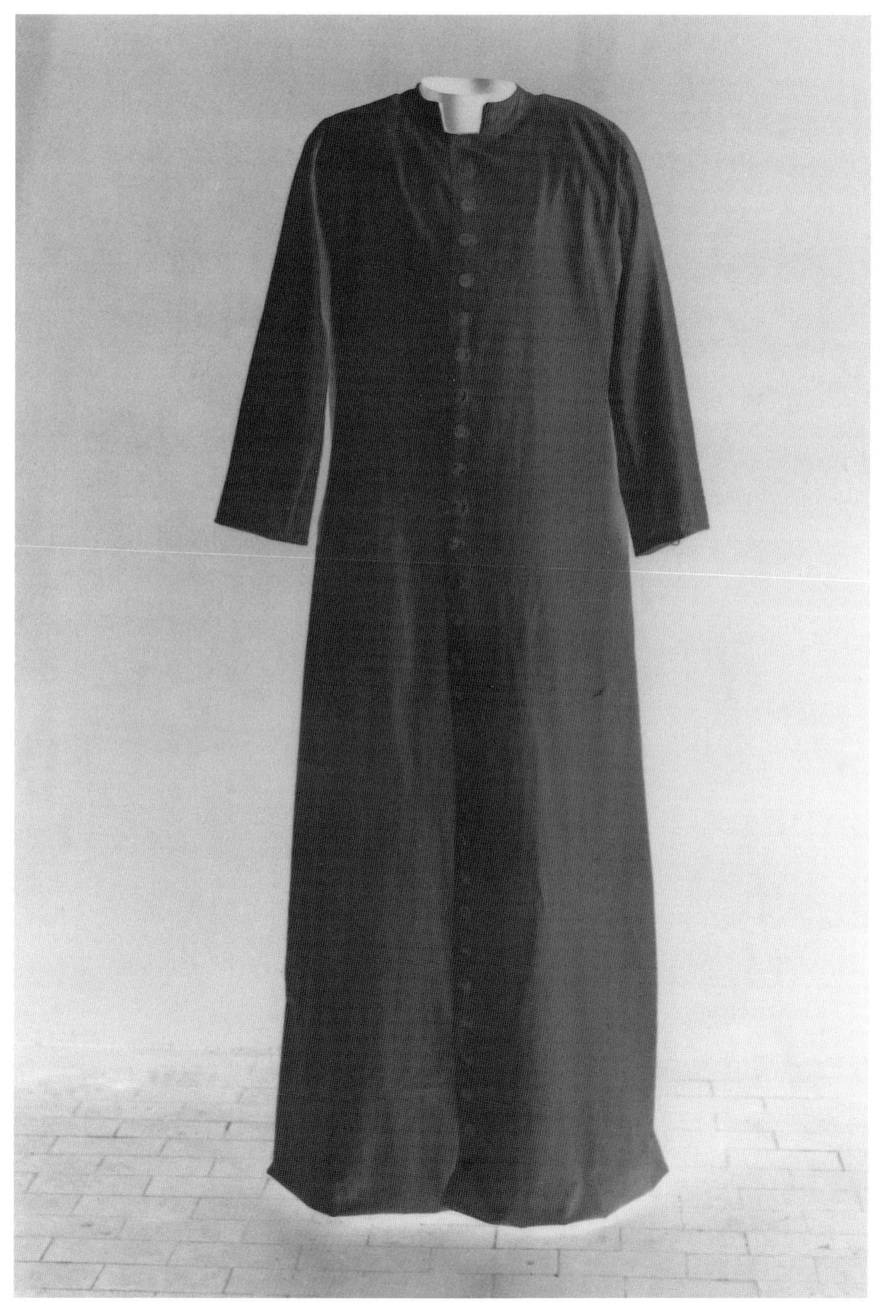

Untitled, 1994

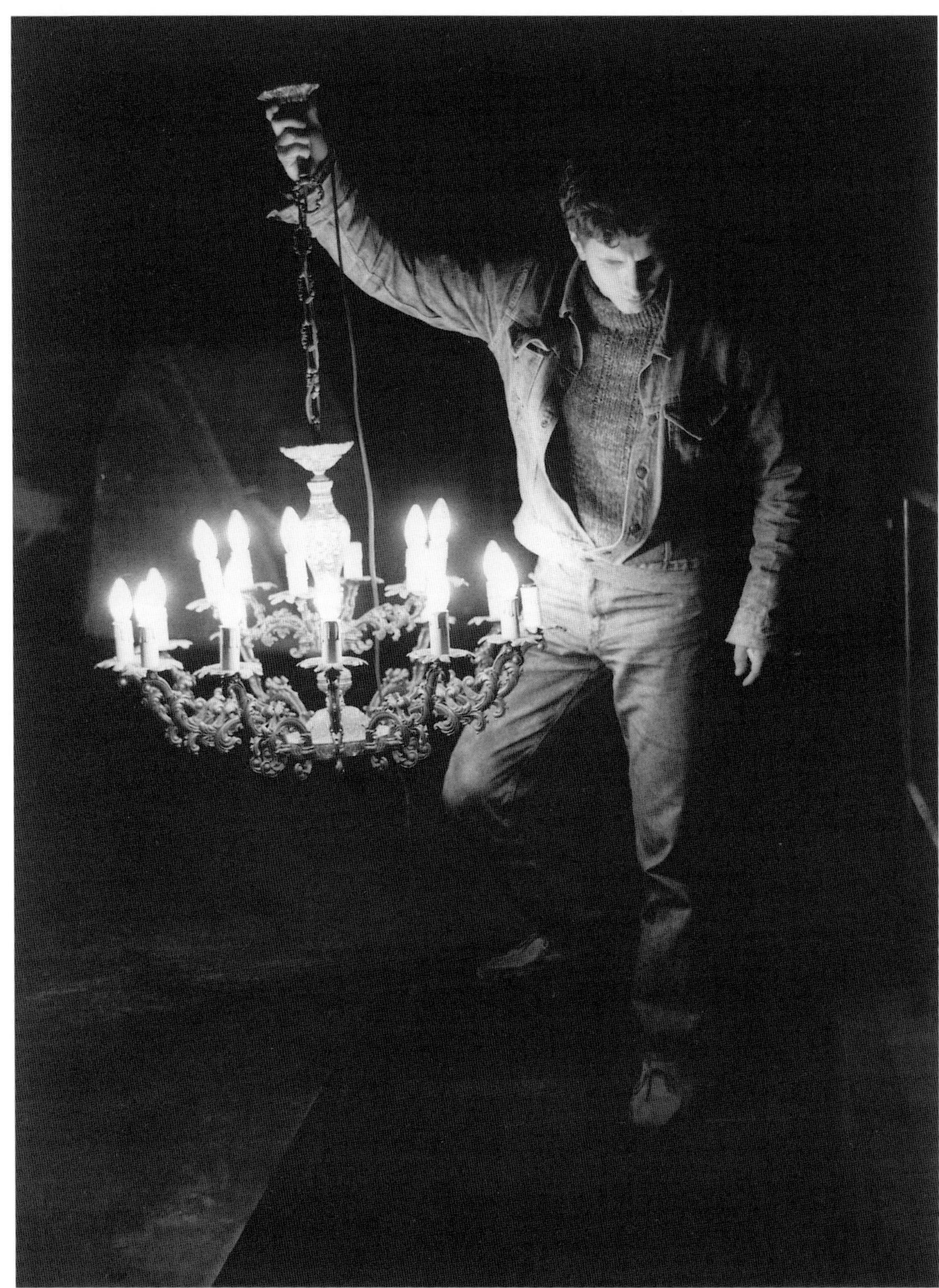

The Stroll, 1994

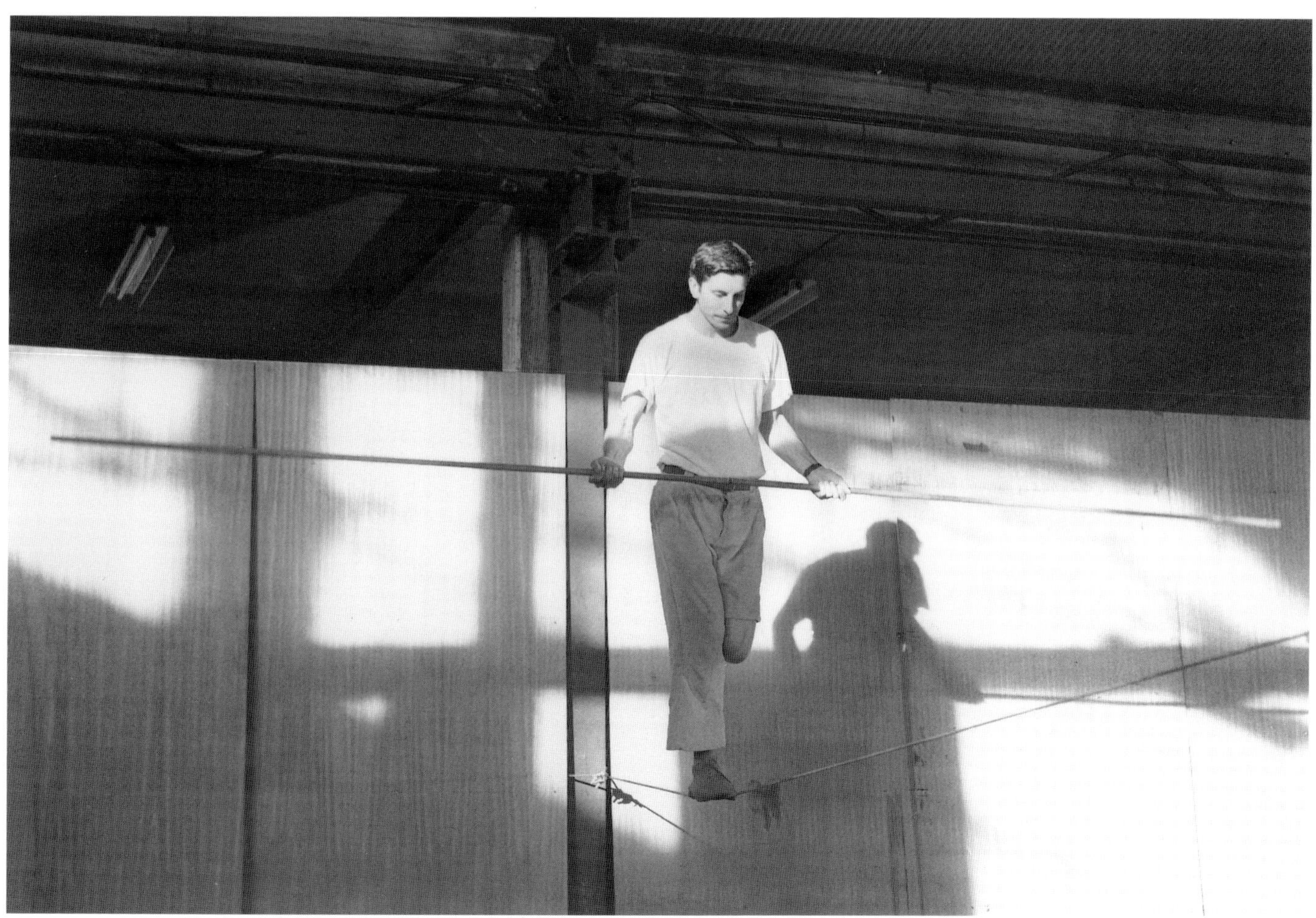

The Stroll II, 1997

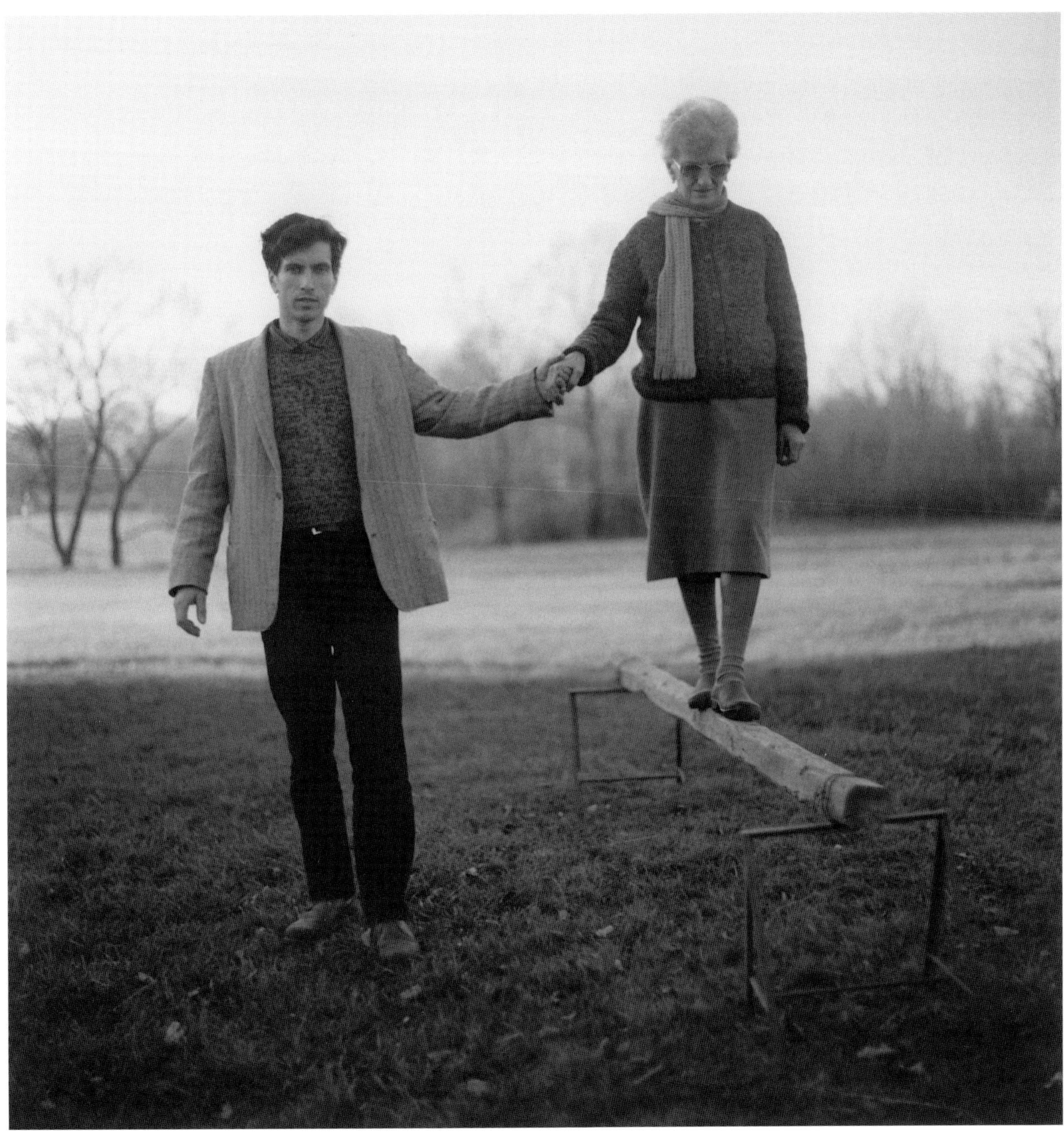

Self-Portrait with Mother, 1996

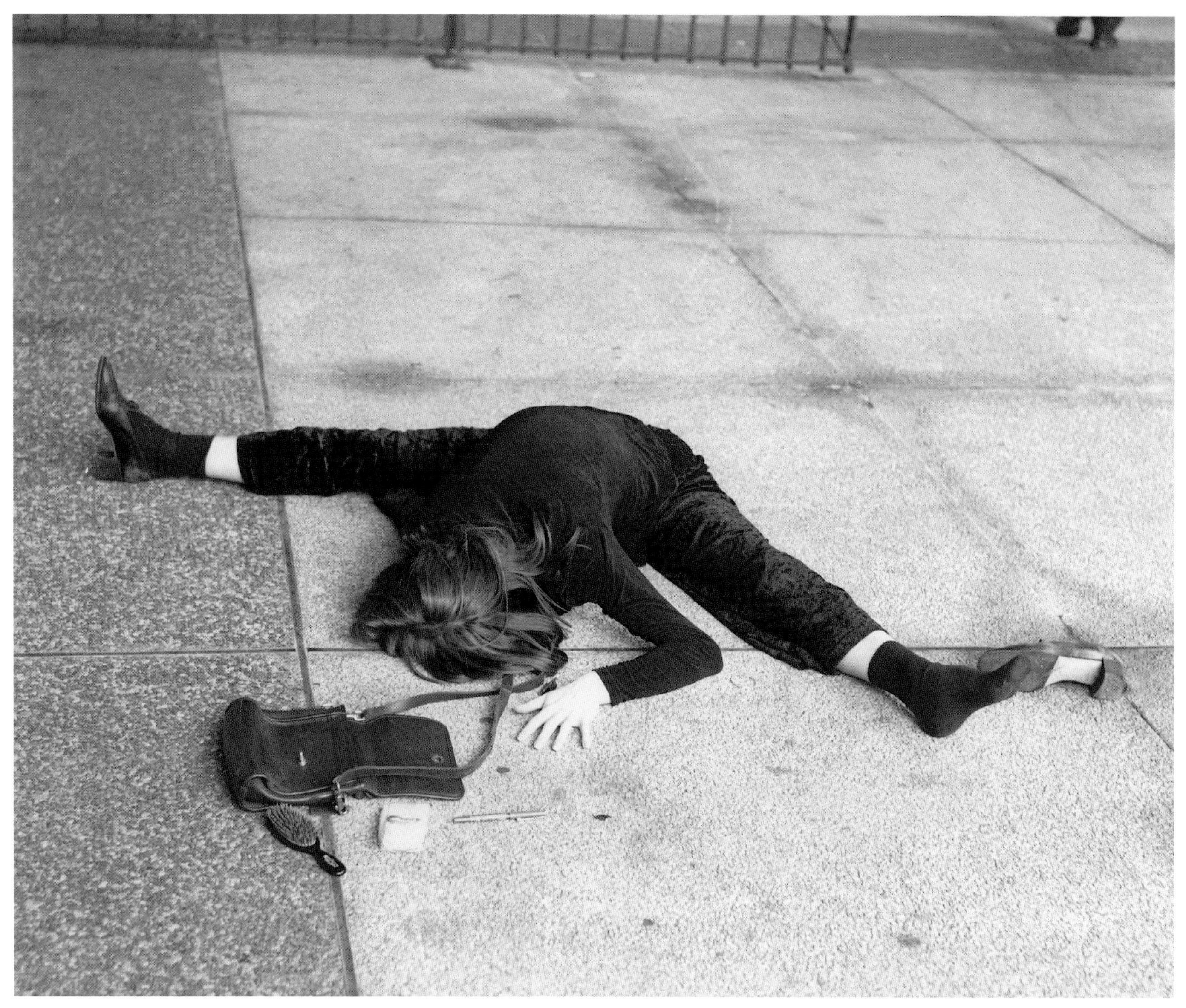

Woman on Sidewalk, 1998

30

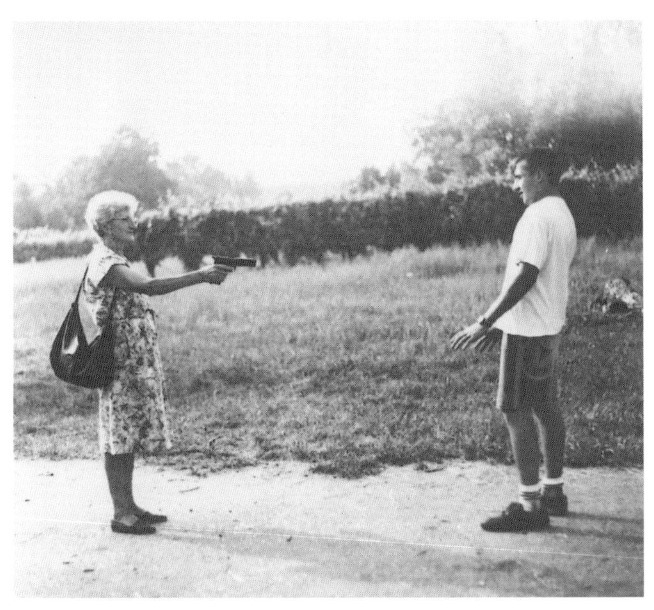
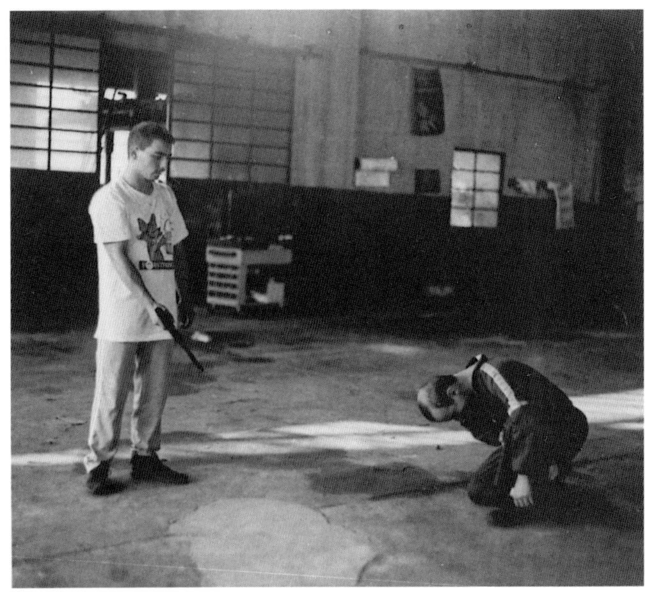
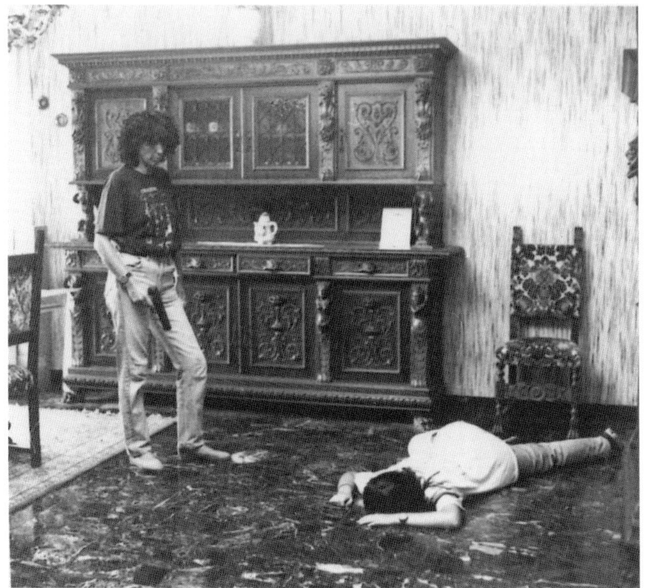
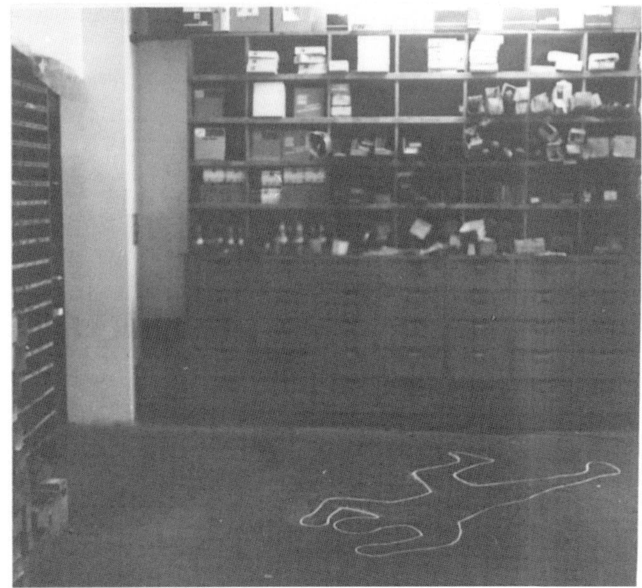

Falling Man, 1995

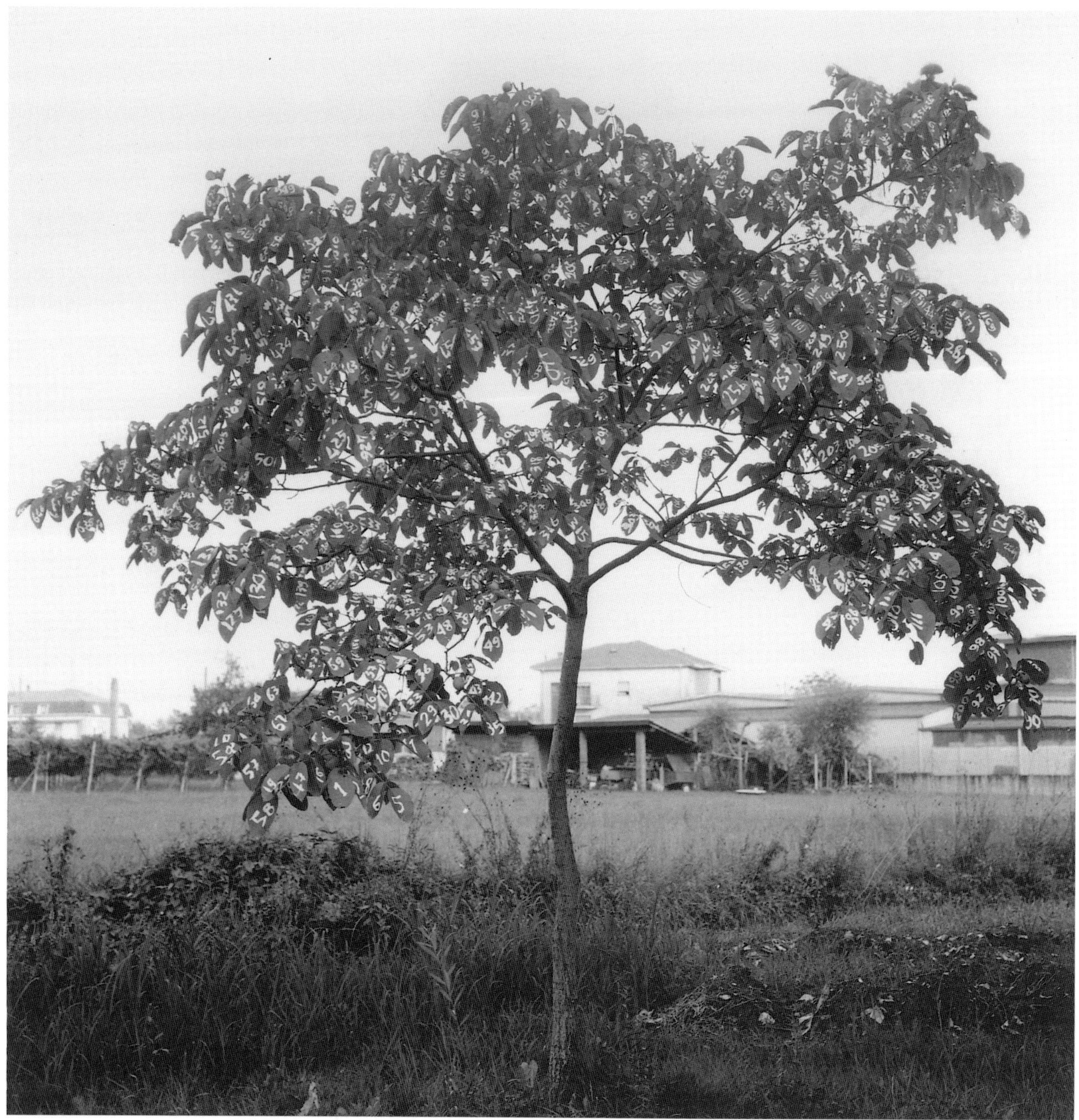

Untitled, 1997

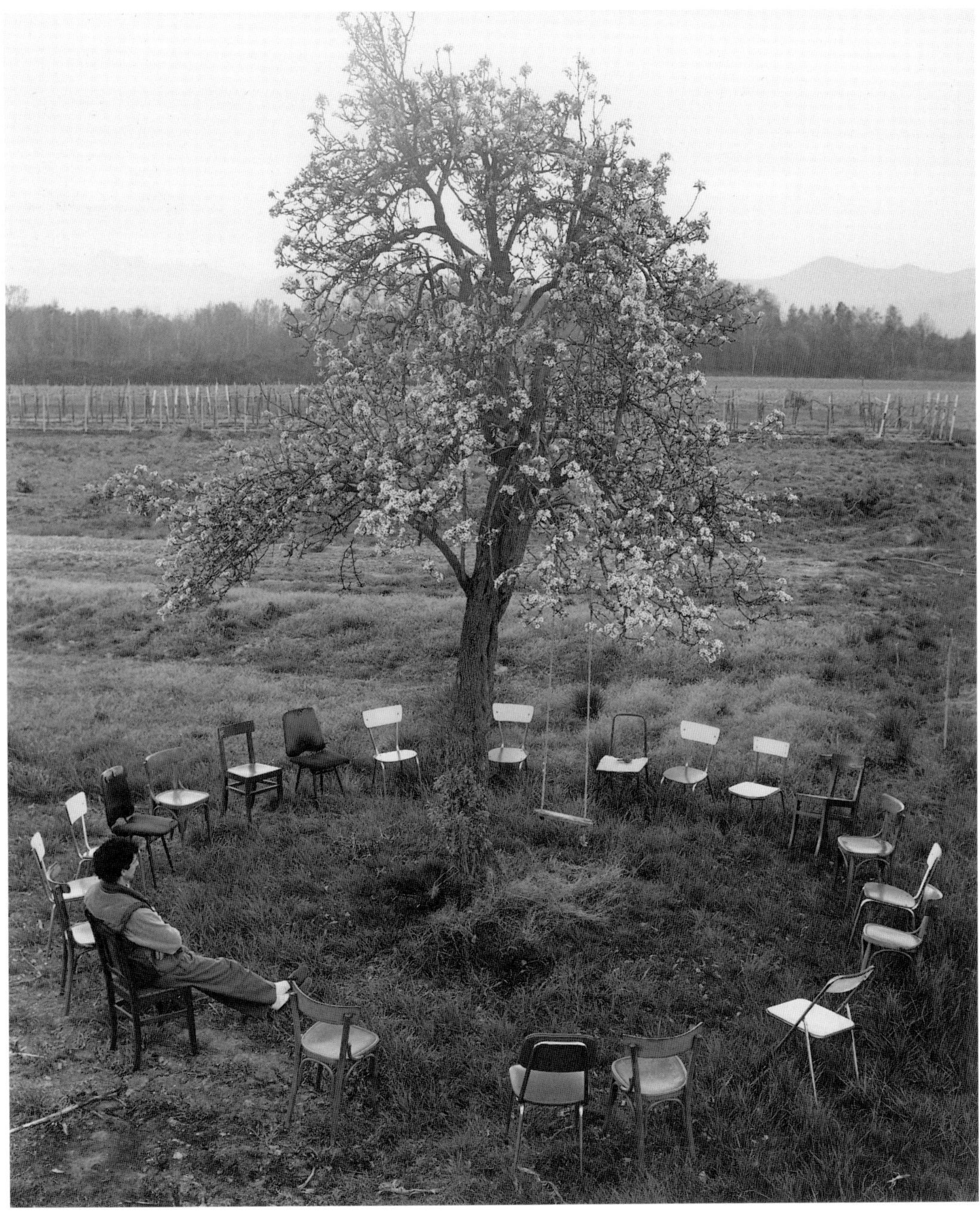

Before the Show, 1995

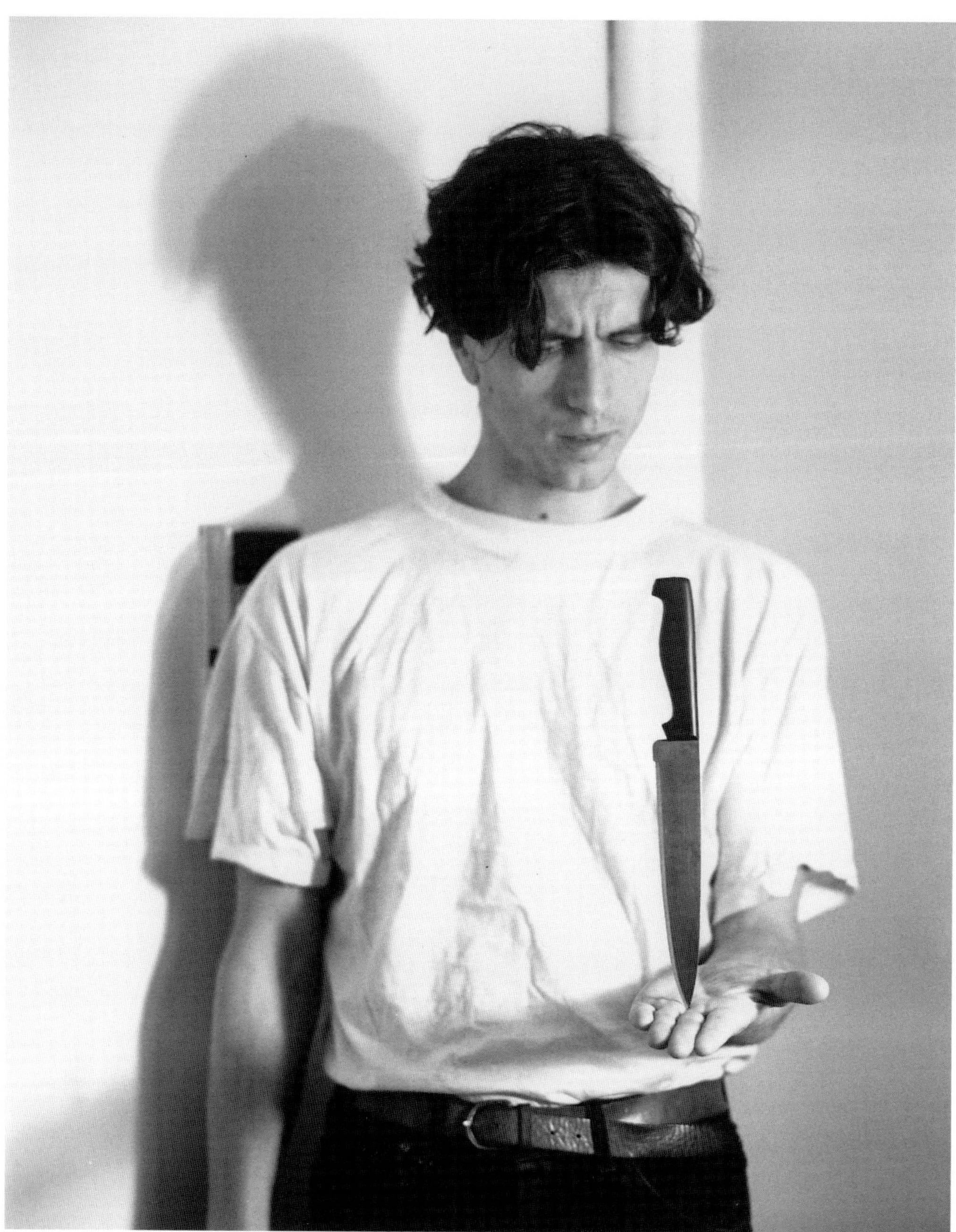

Self-Portrait, 1995

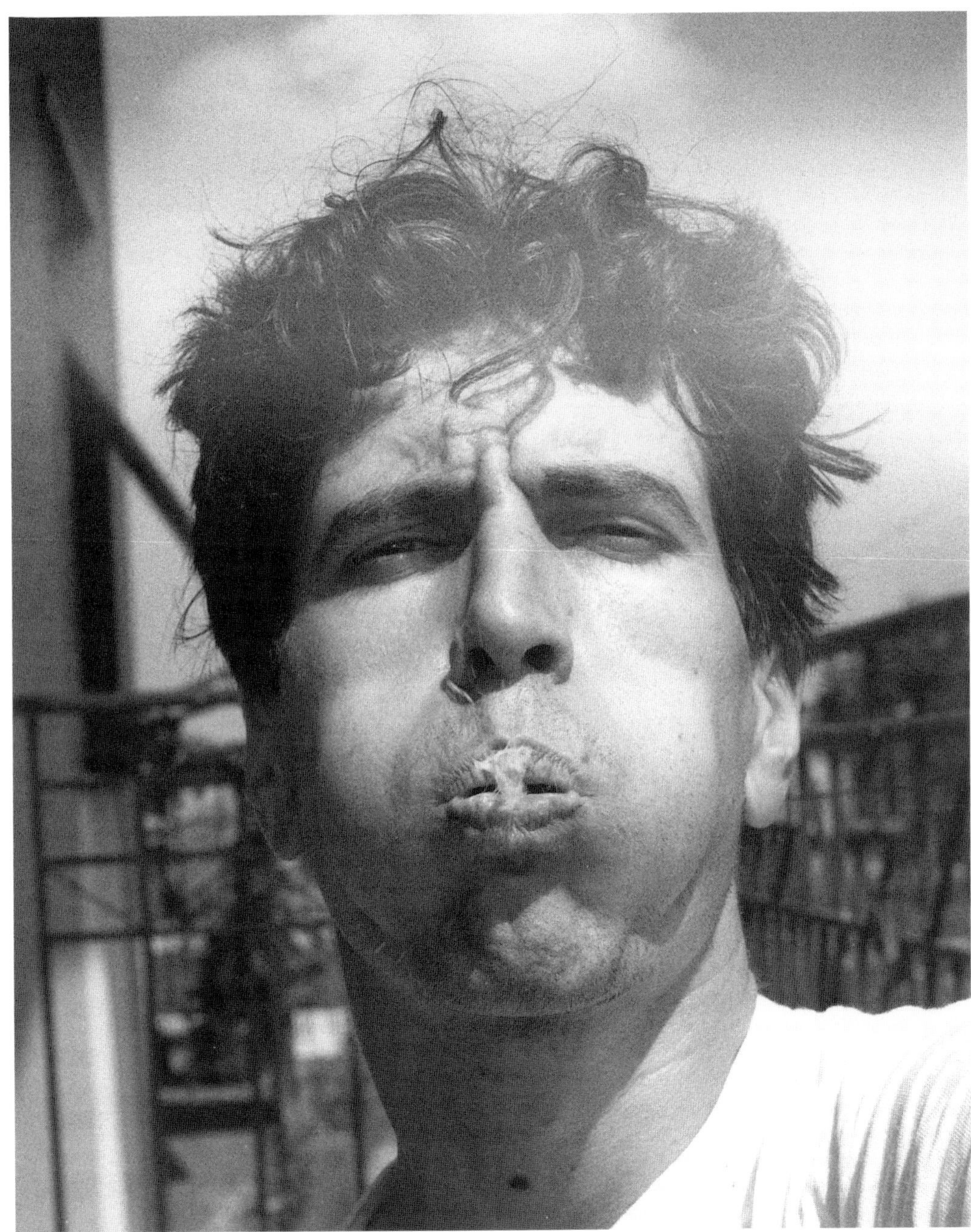

Self-Portrait, 1995

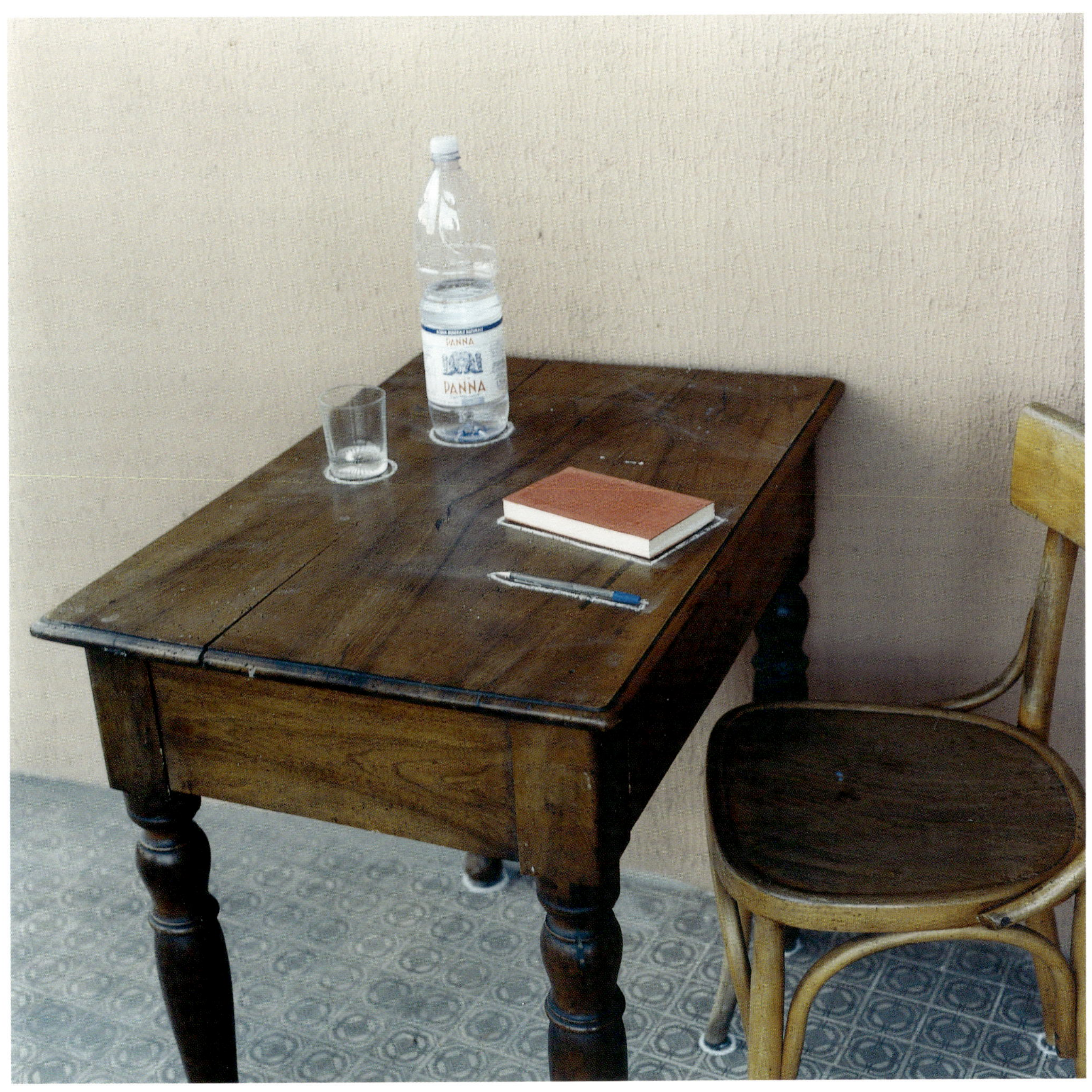

More than Still, 2001

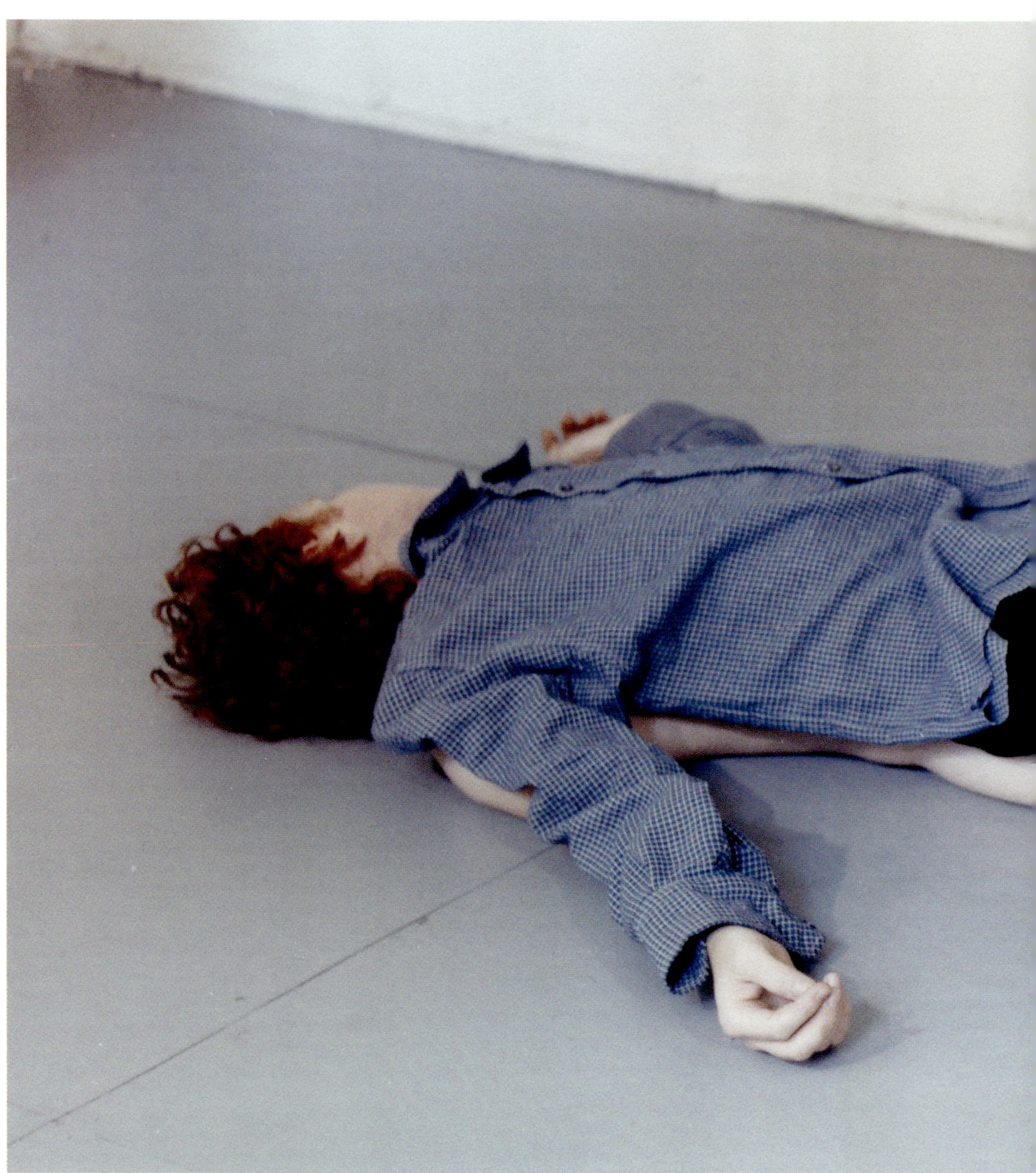

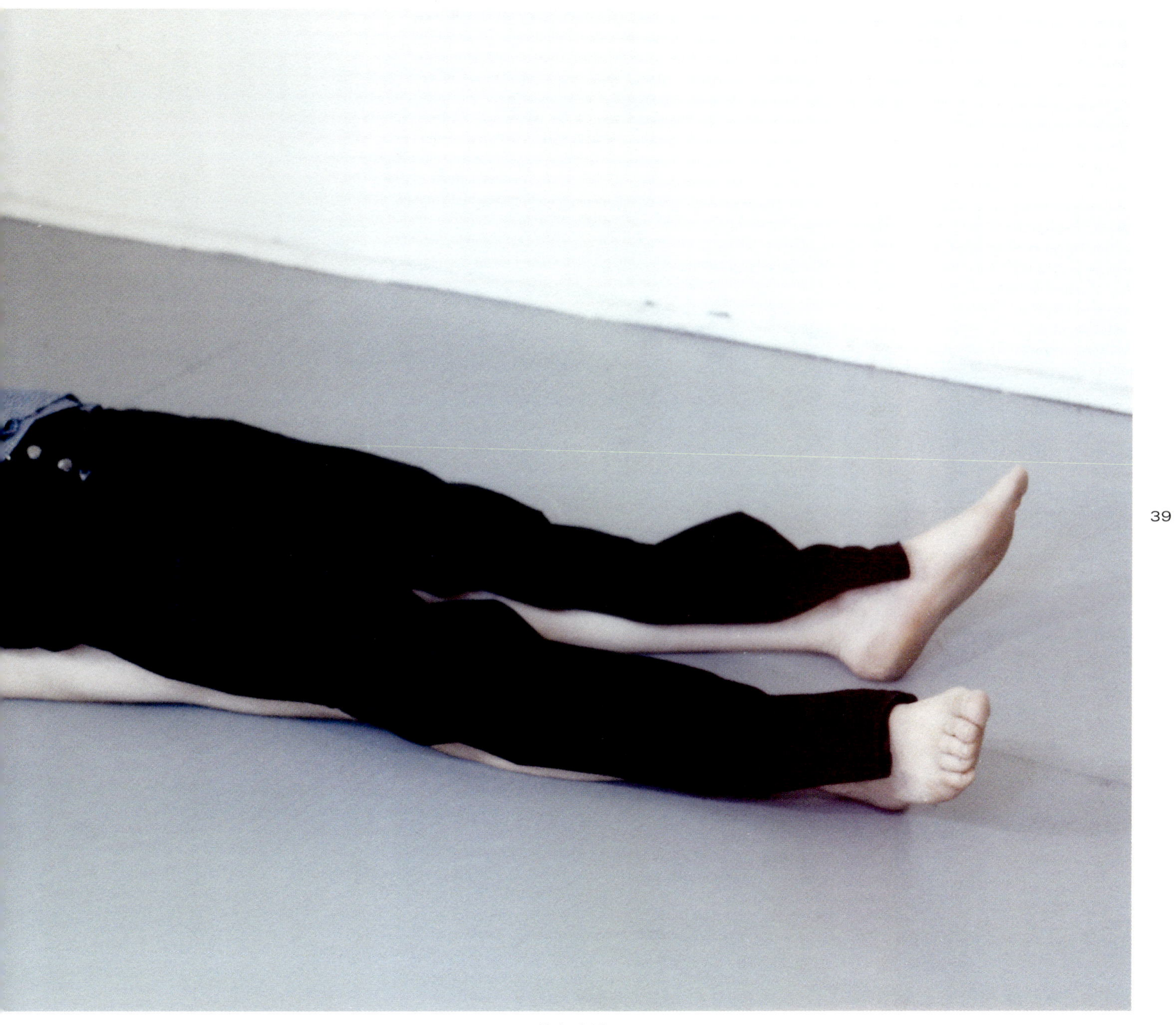

Naked Man, 1998

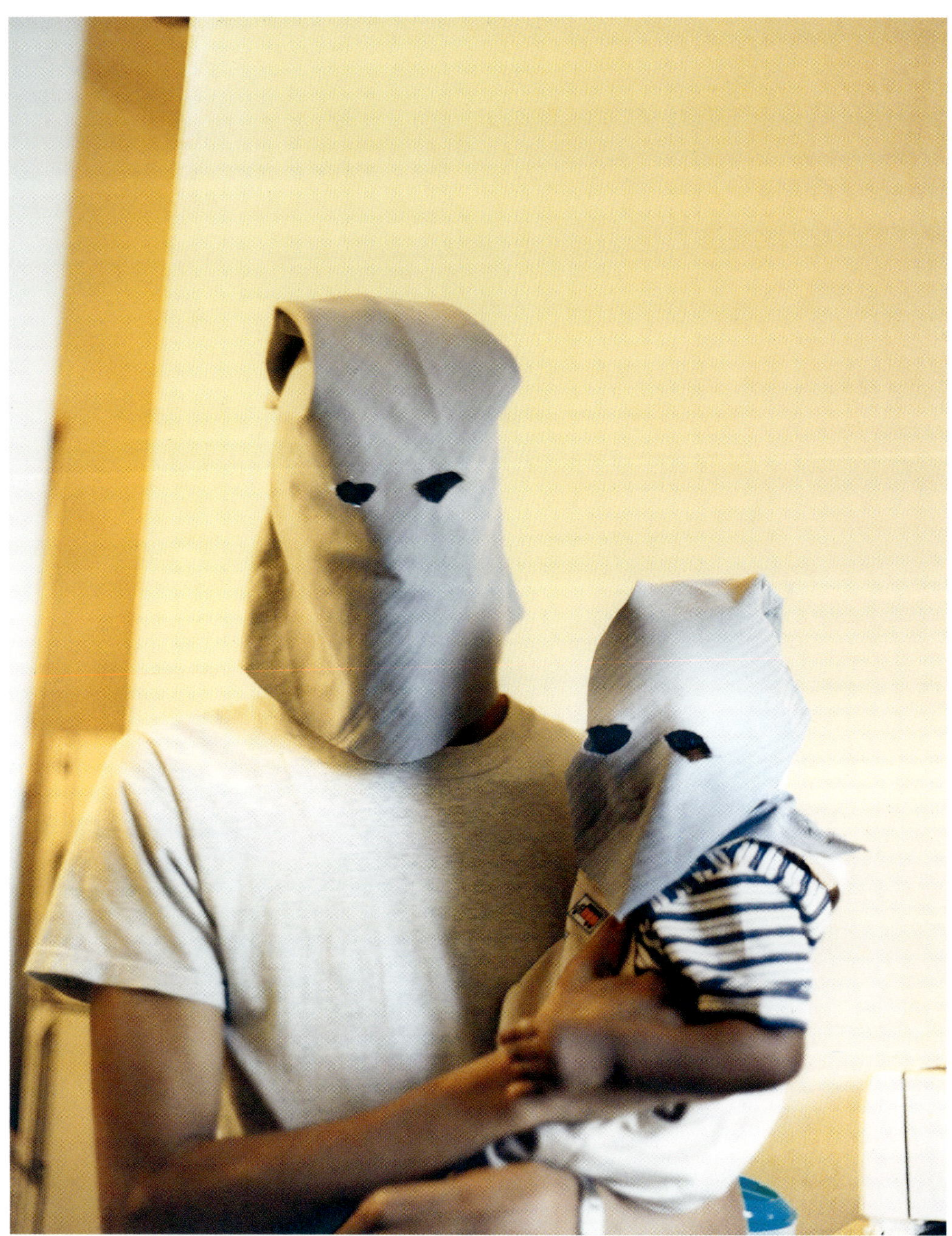

Man and Baby, 2001

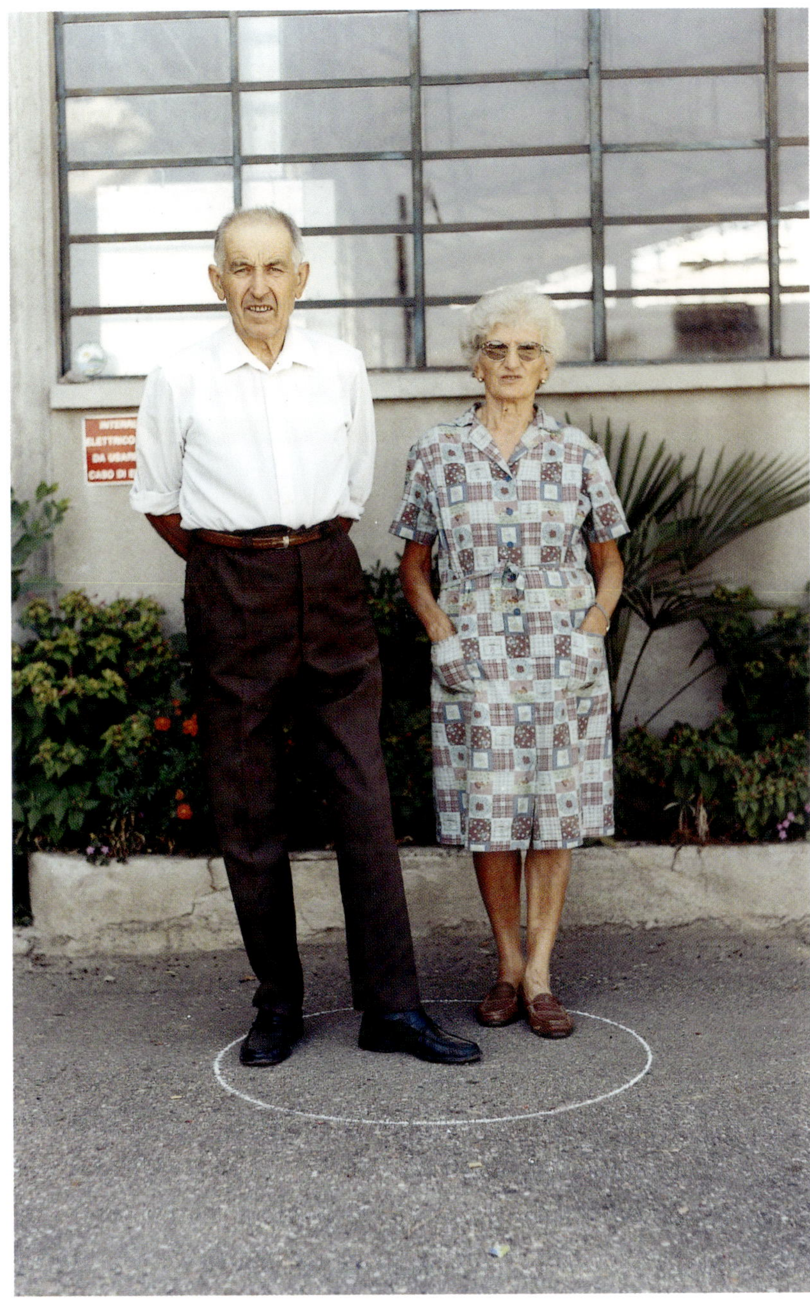

Portrait of My Parents, 2001

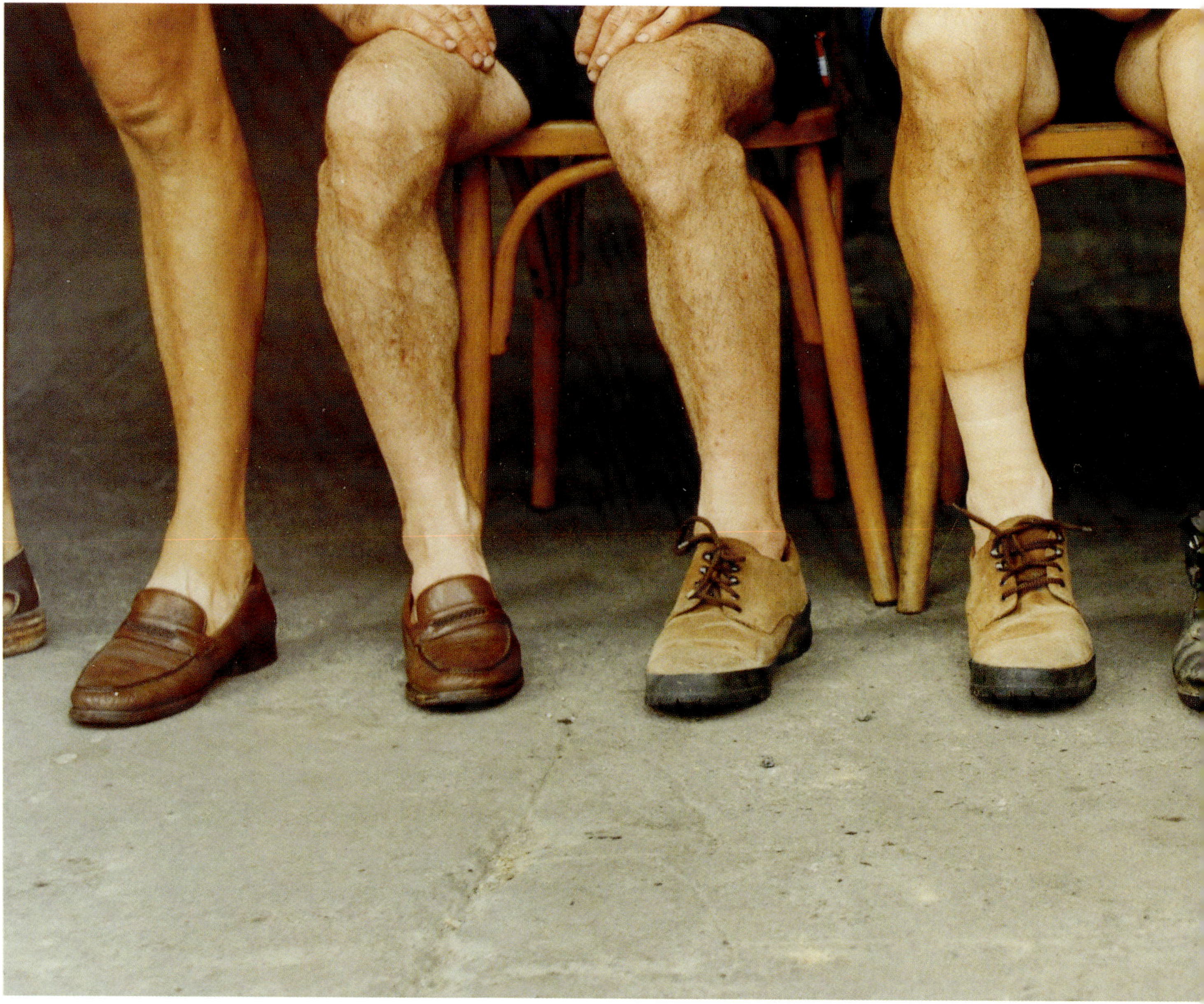

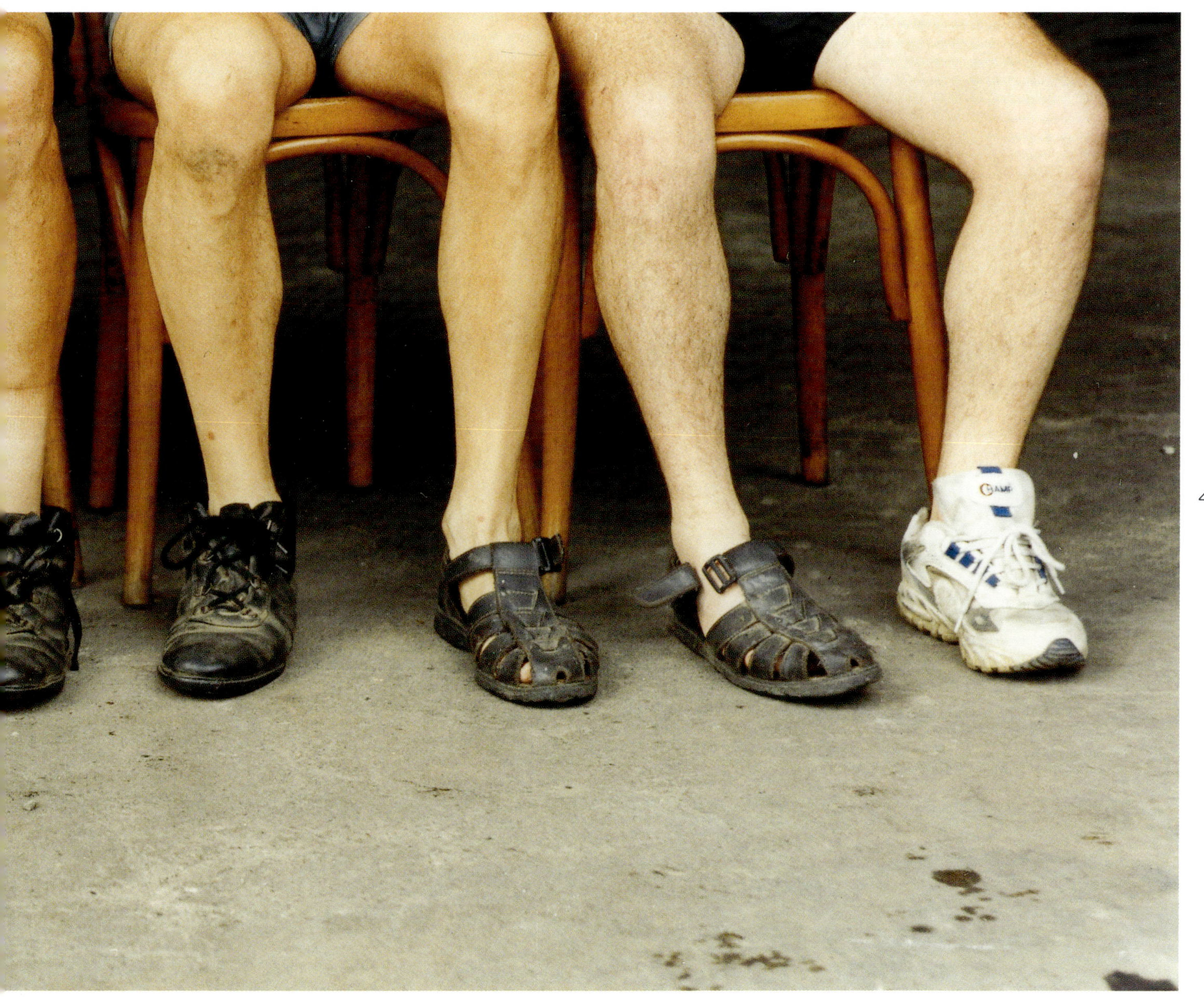

Feet and Shoes, 2000

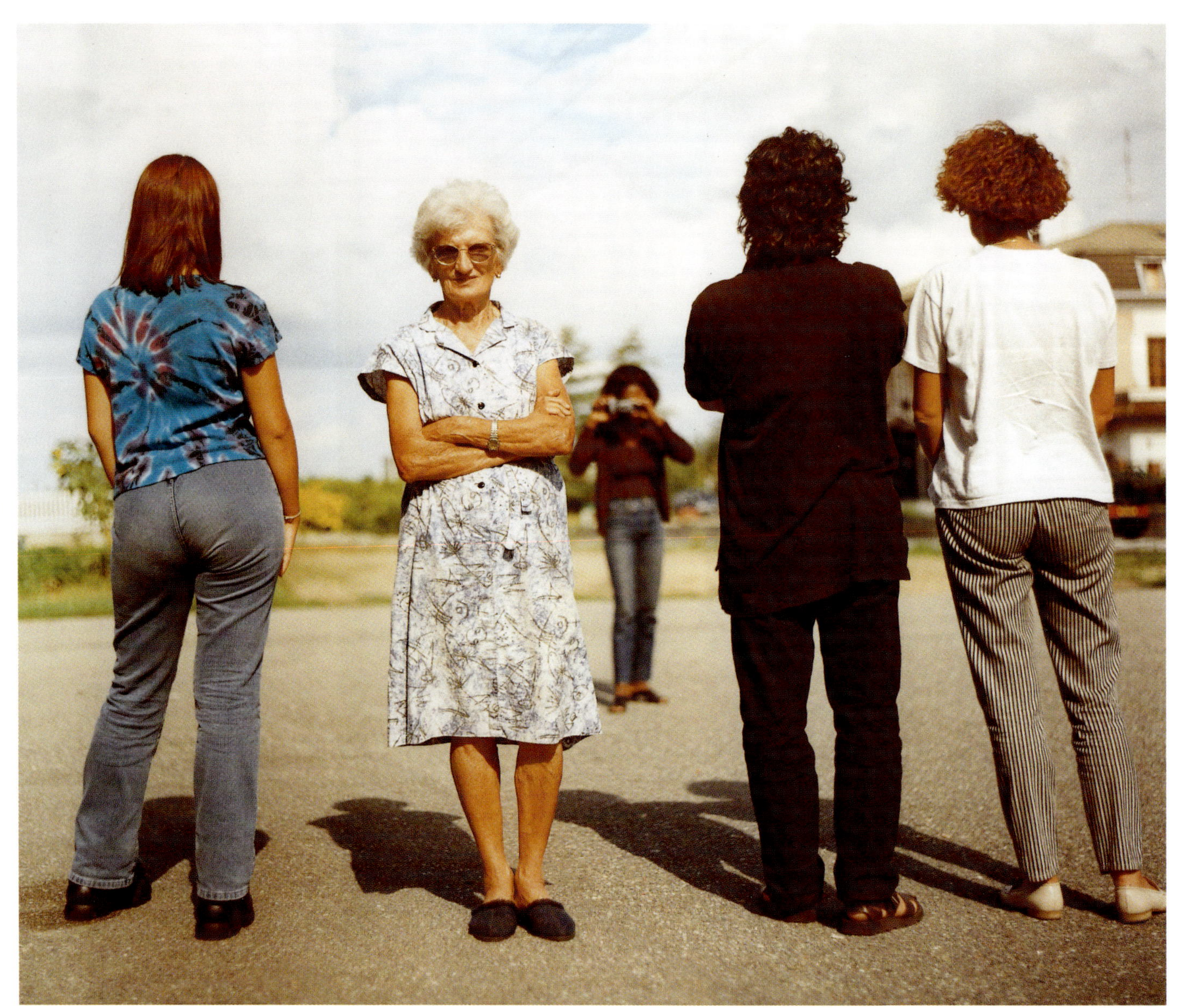

44

Portrait of Mother, 2000

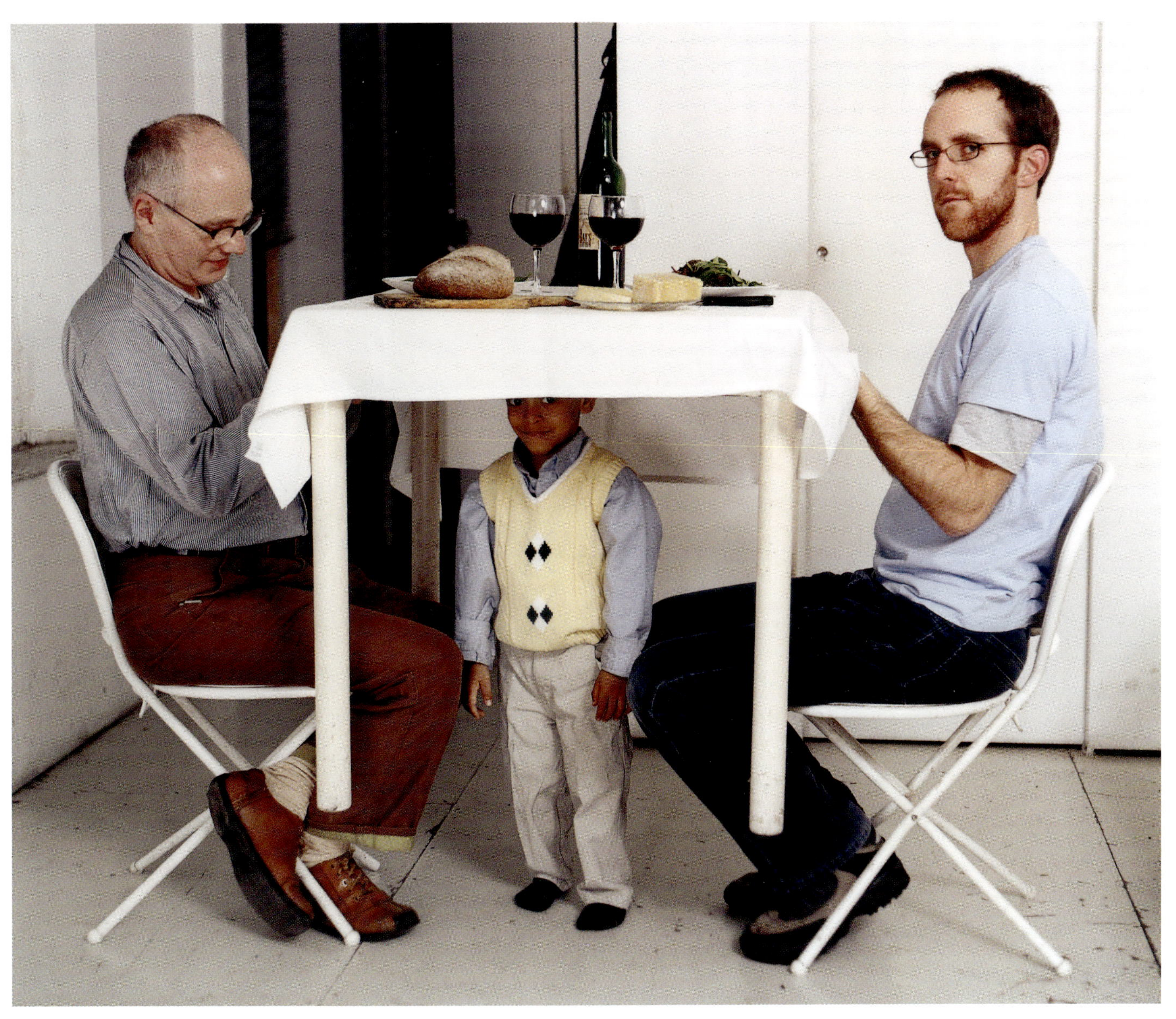

Untitled, 2005

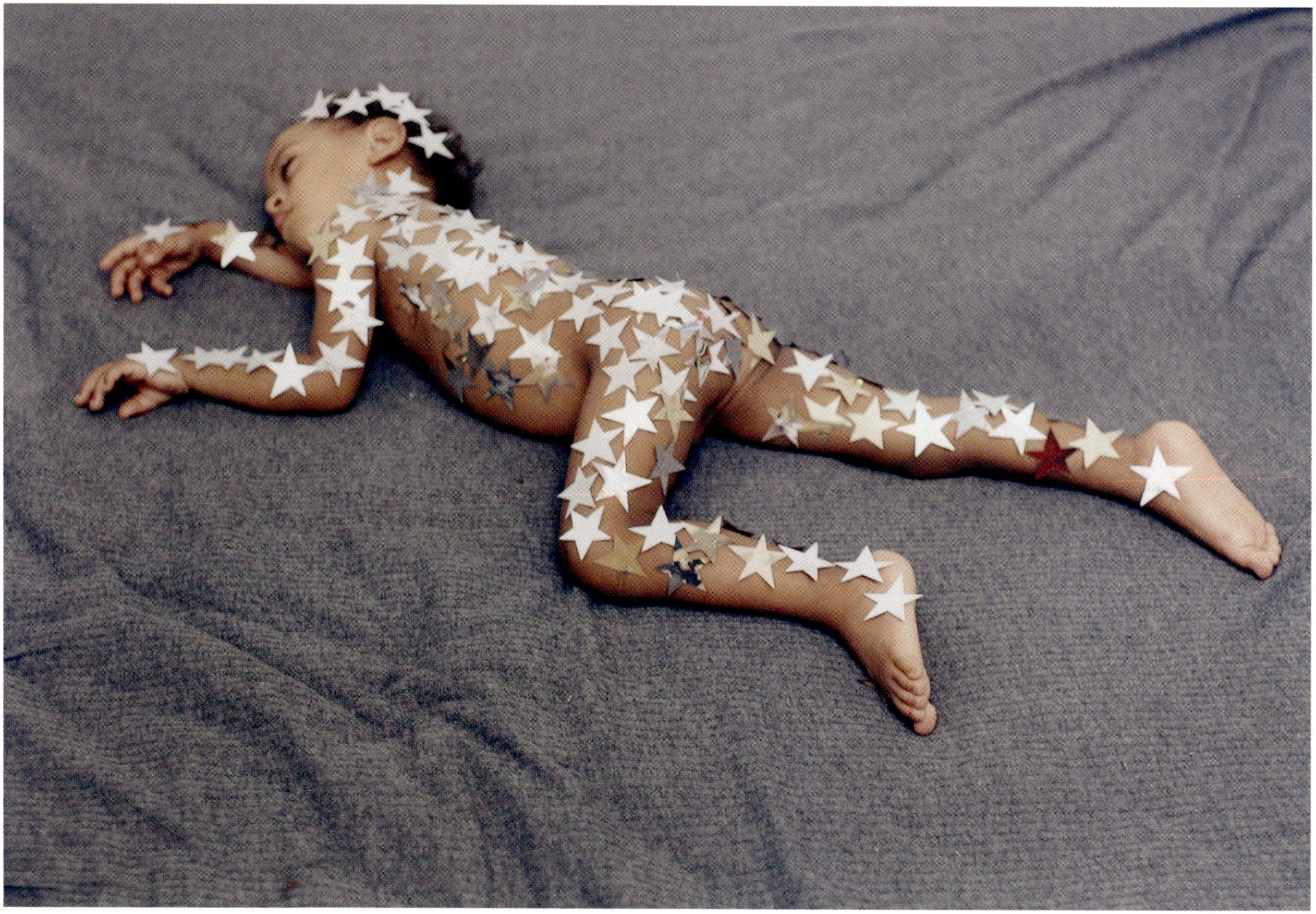

Untitled, 2004

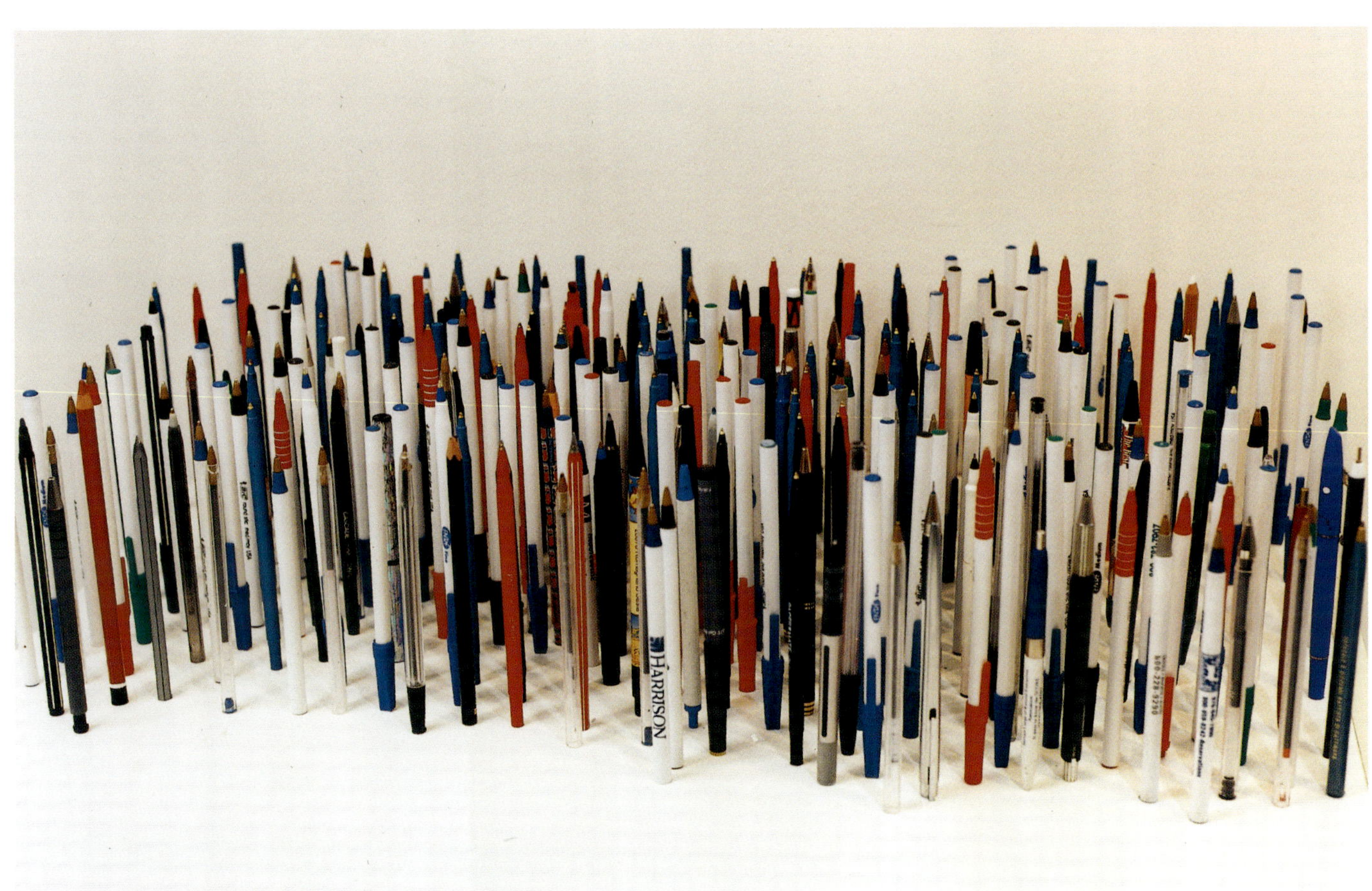

My Pen Collection, 2001

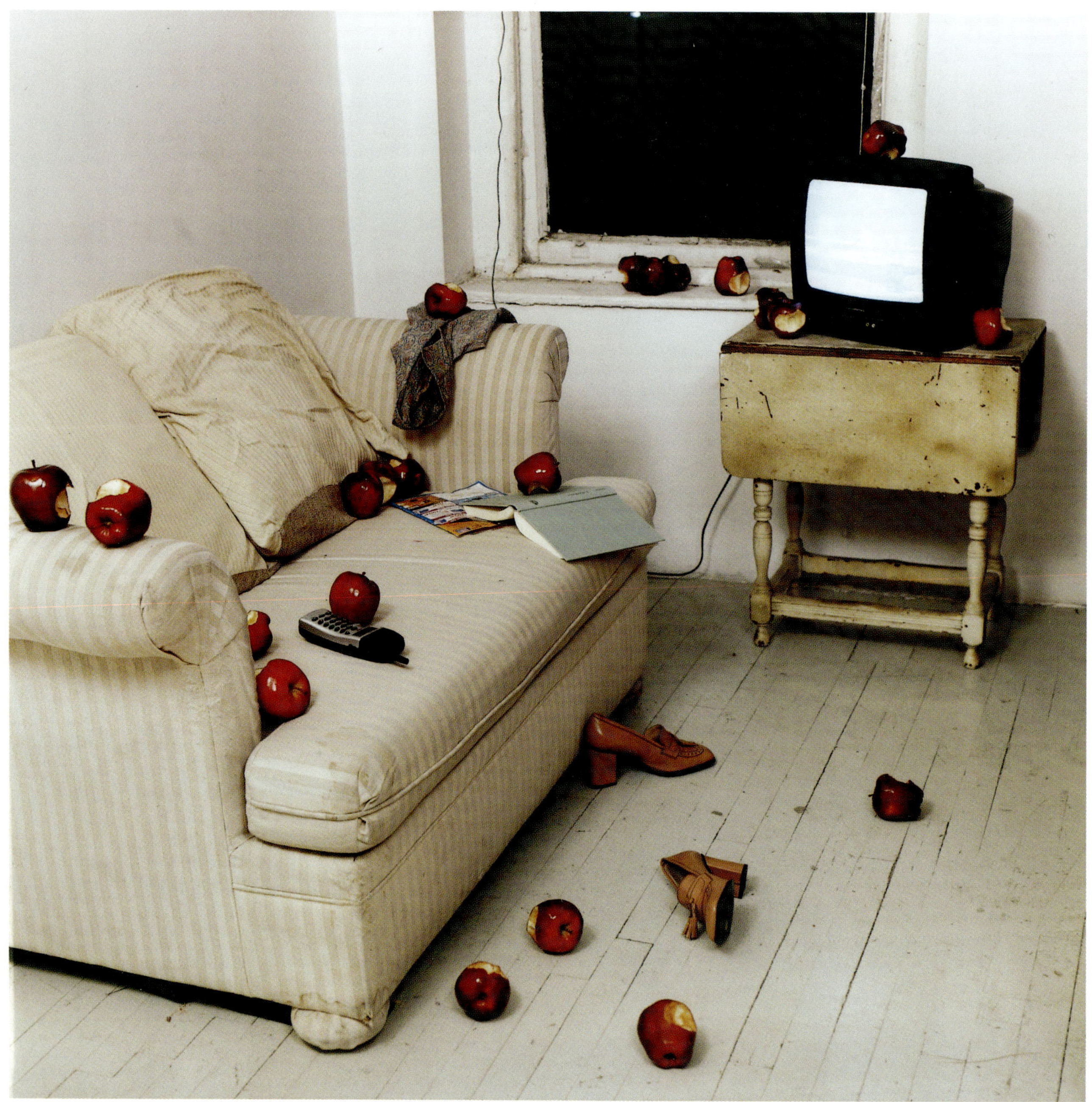

Saturday Night, 2003

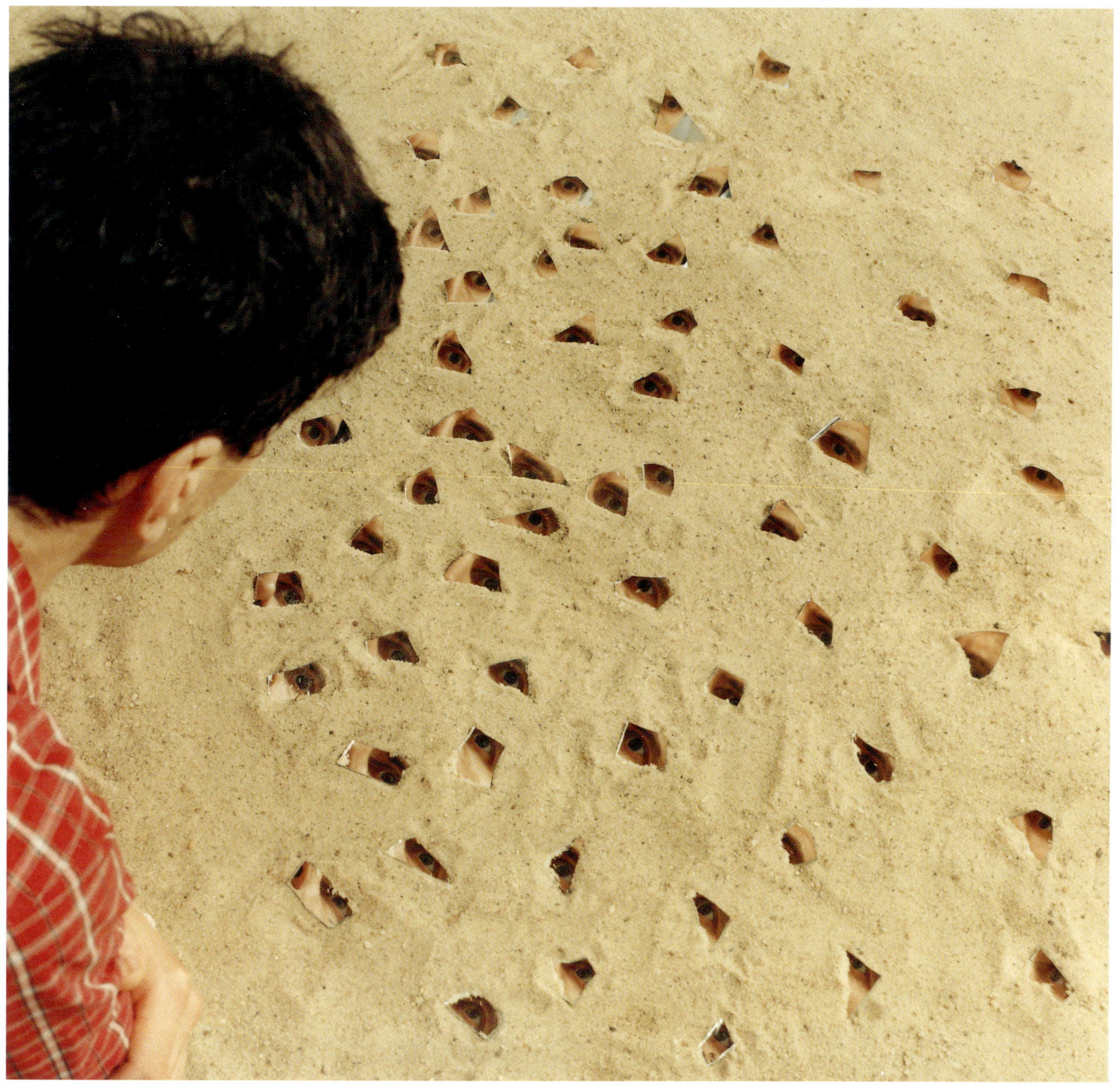

On the Beach, 2002

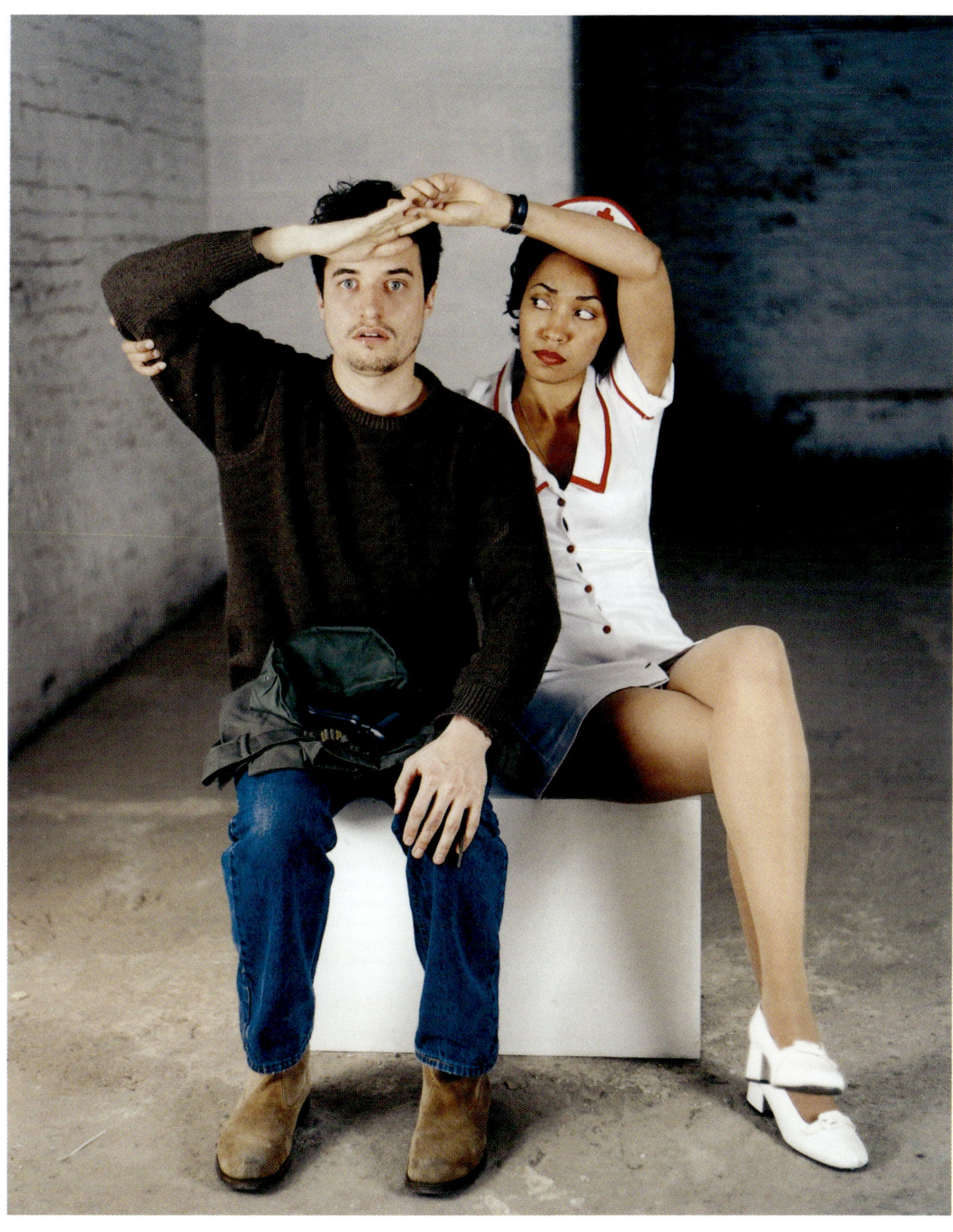

Eastern Standard Time, 2005

51

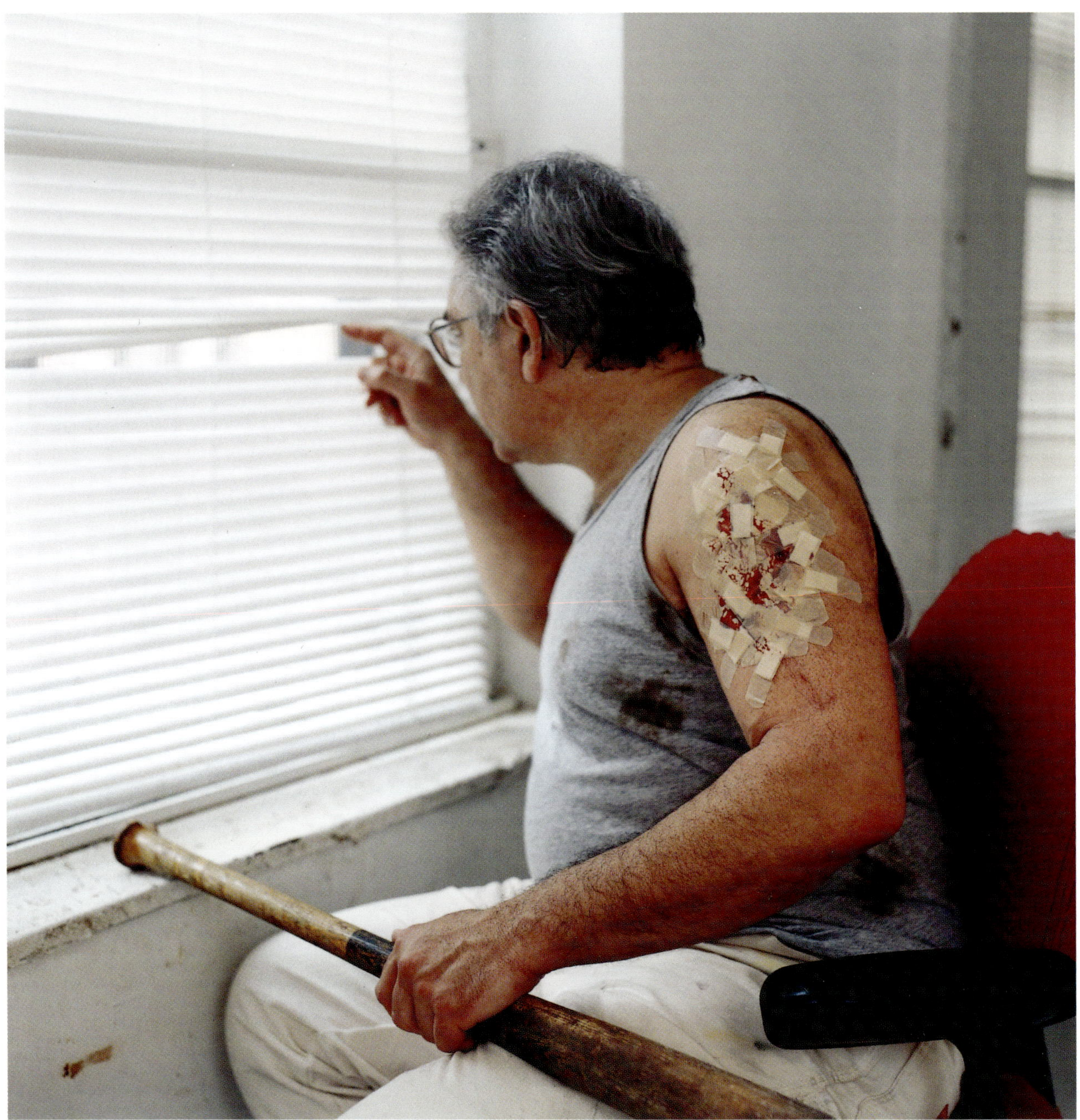

Man in Front of the Window, 2004

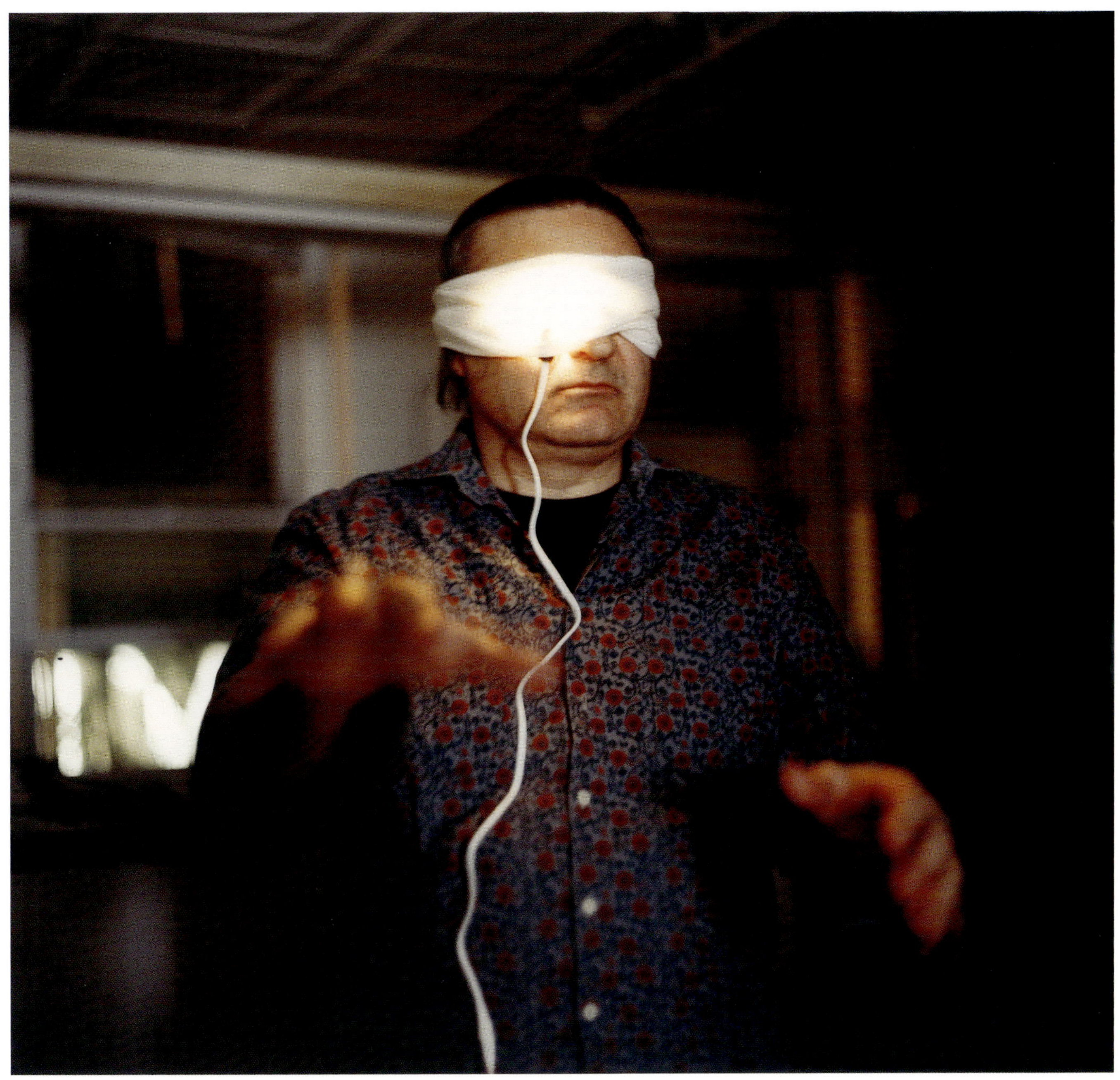

Untitled, 2005

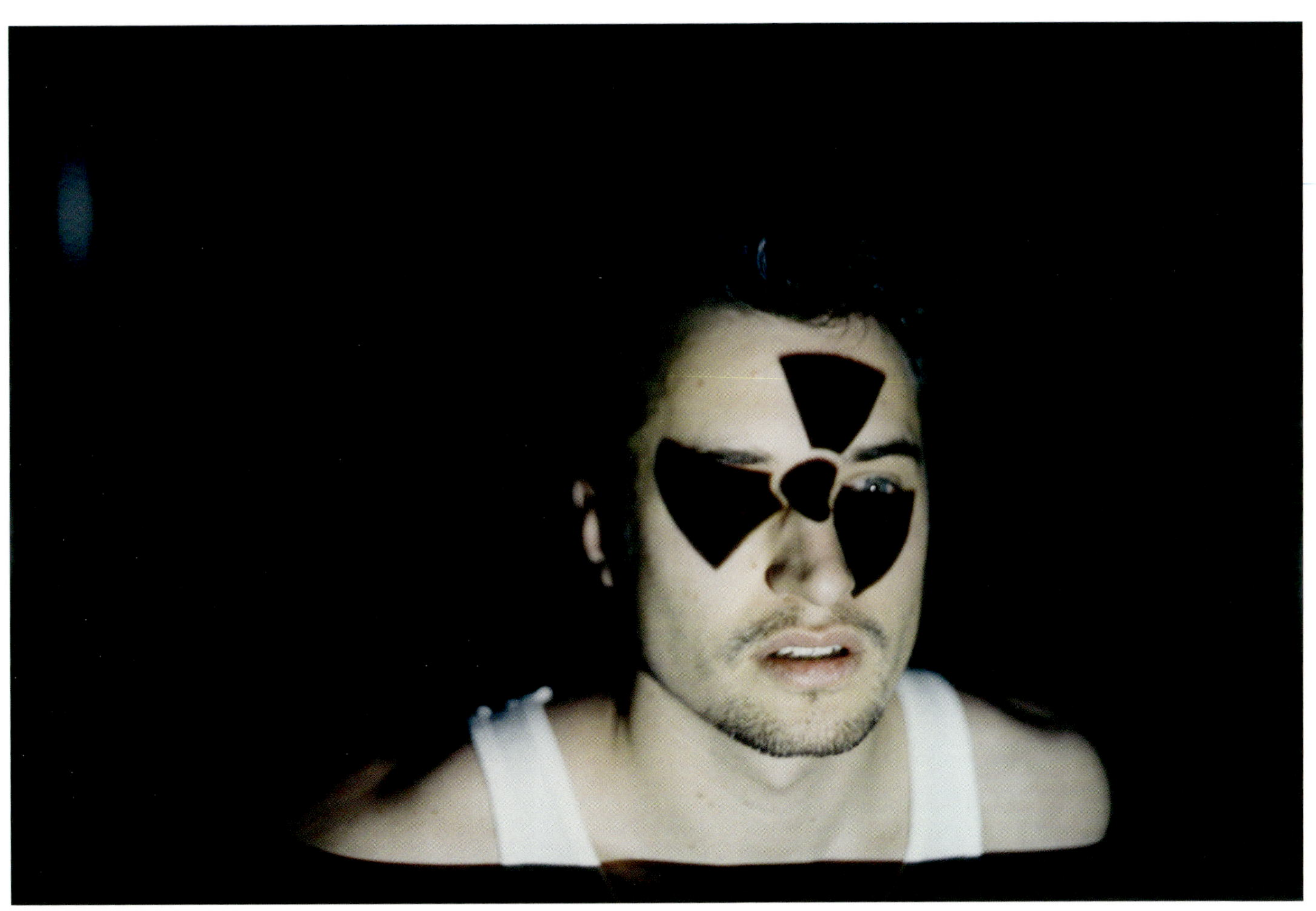

Spelling, 2005

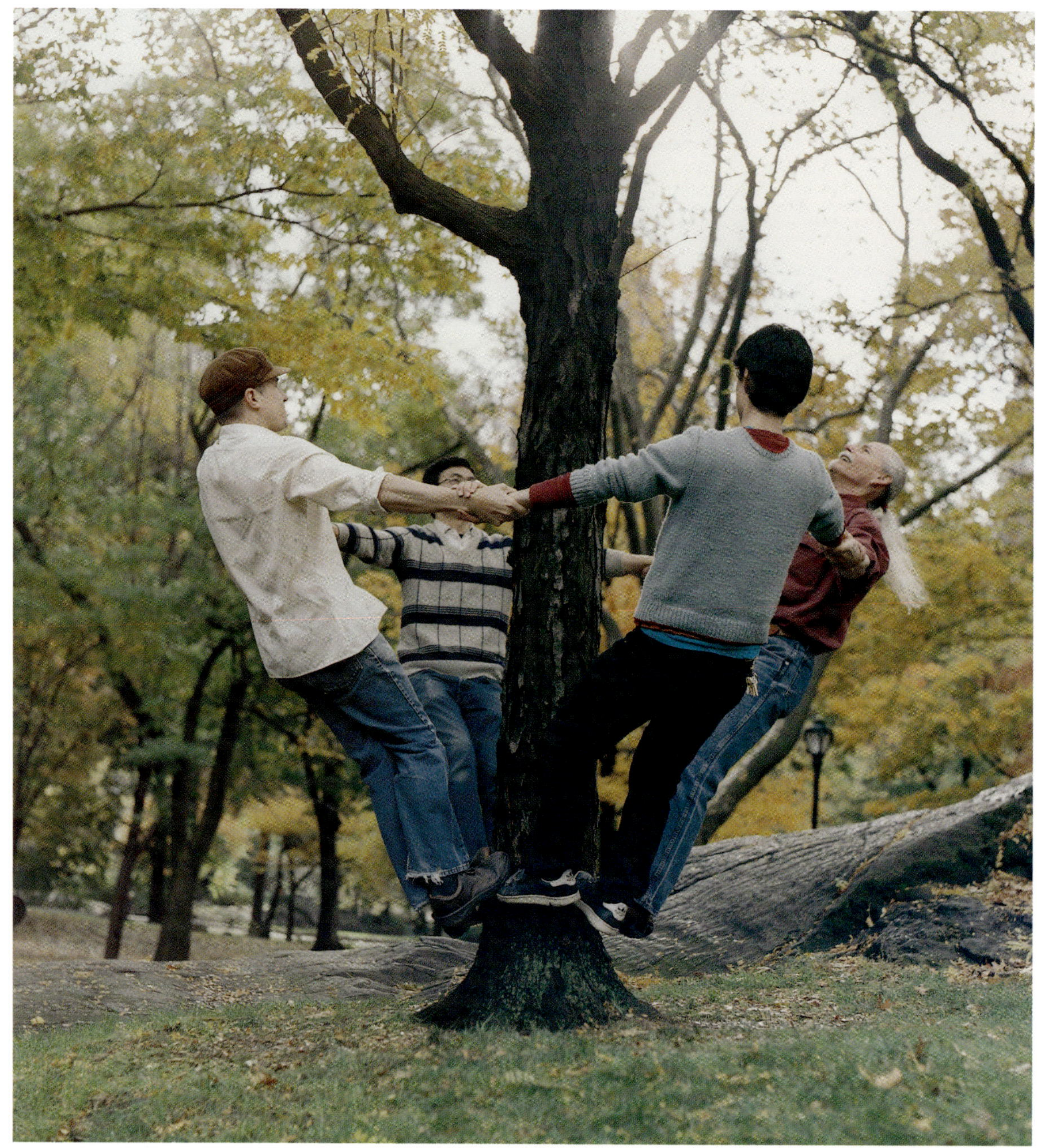

My Four Friends, 2006

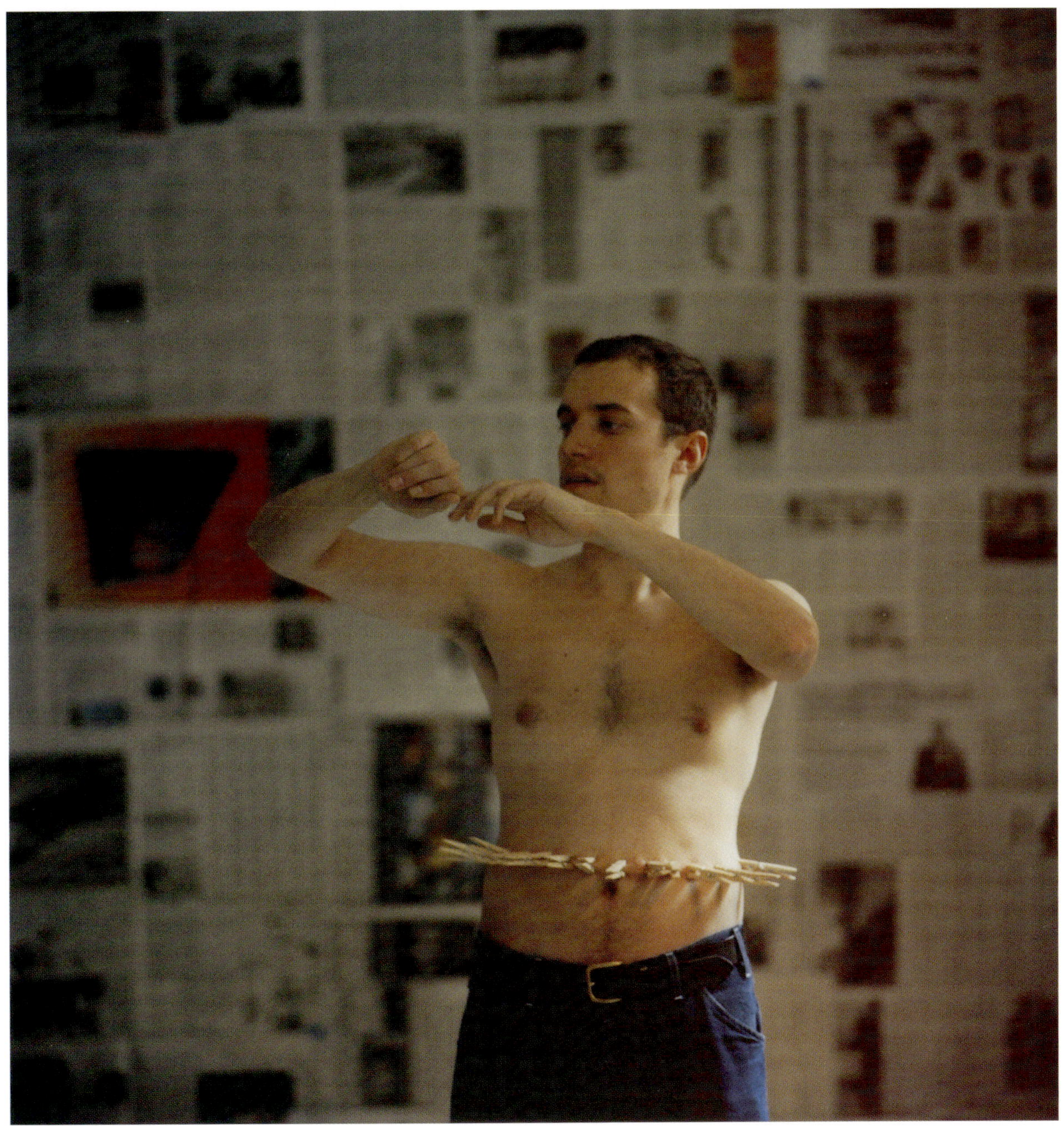

Untitled, 2006

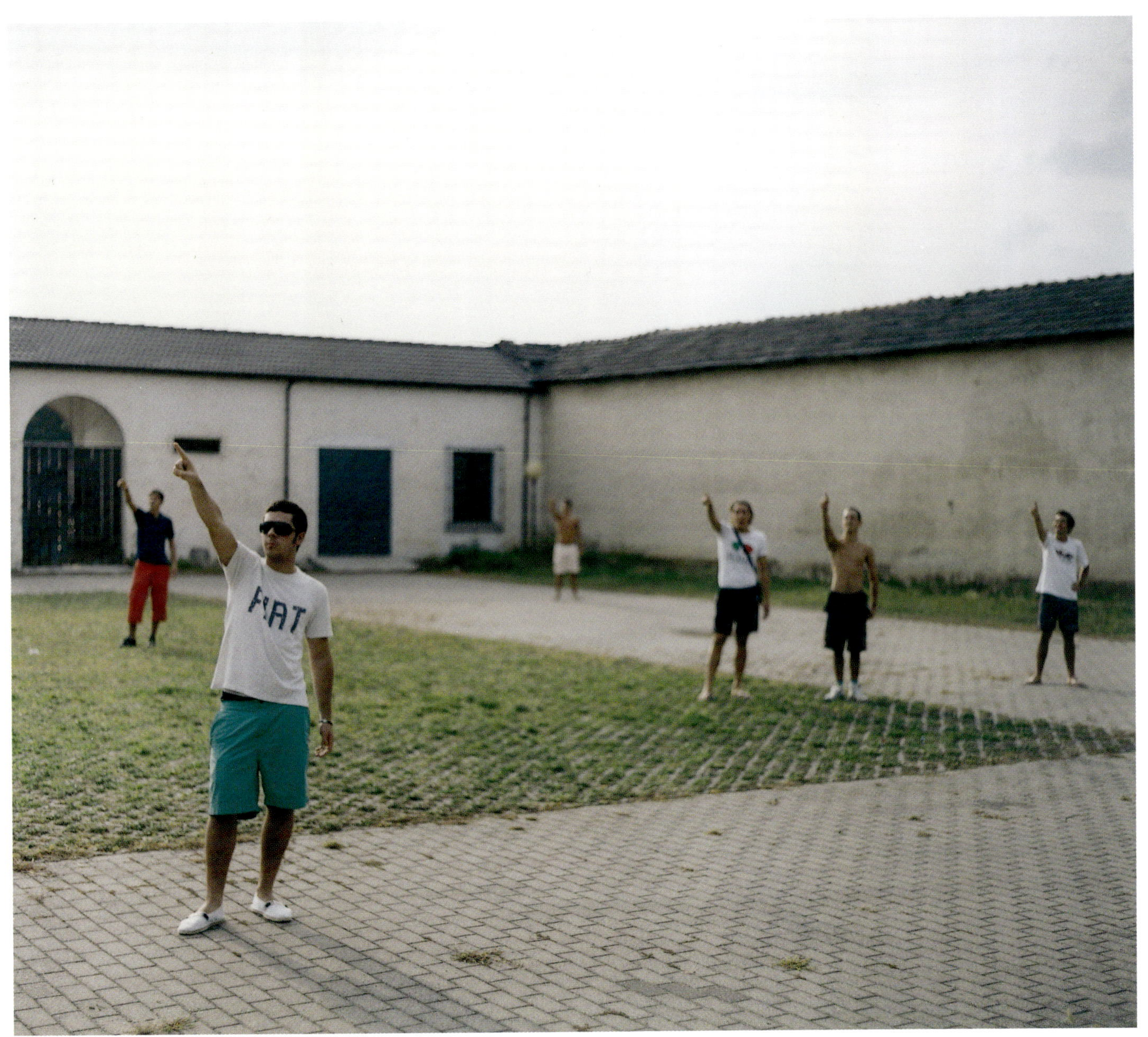

Untitled, 2006

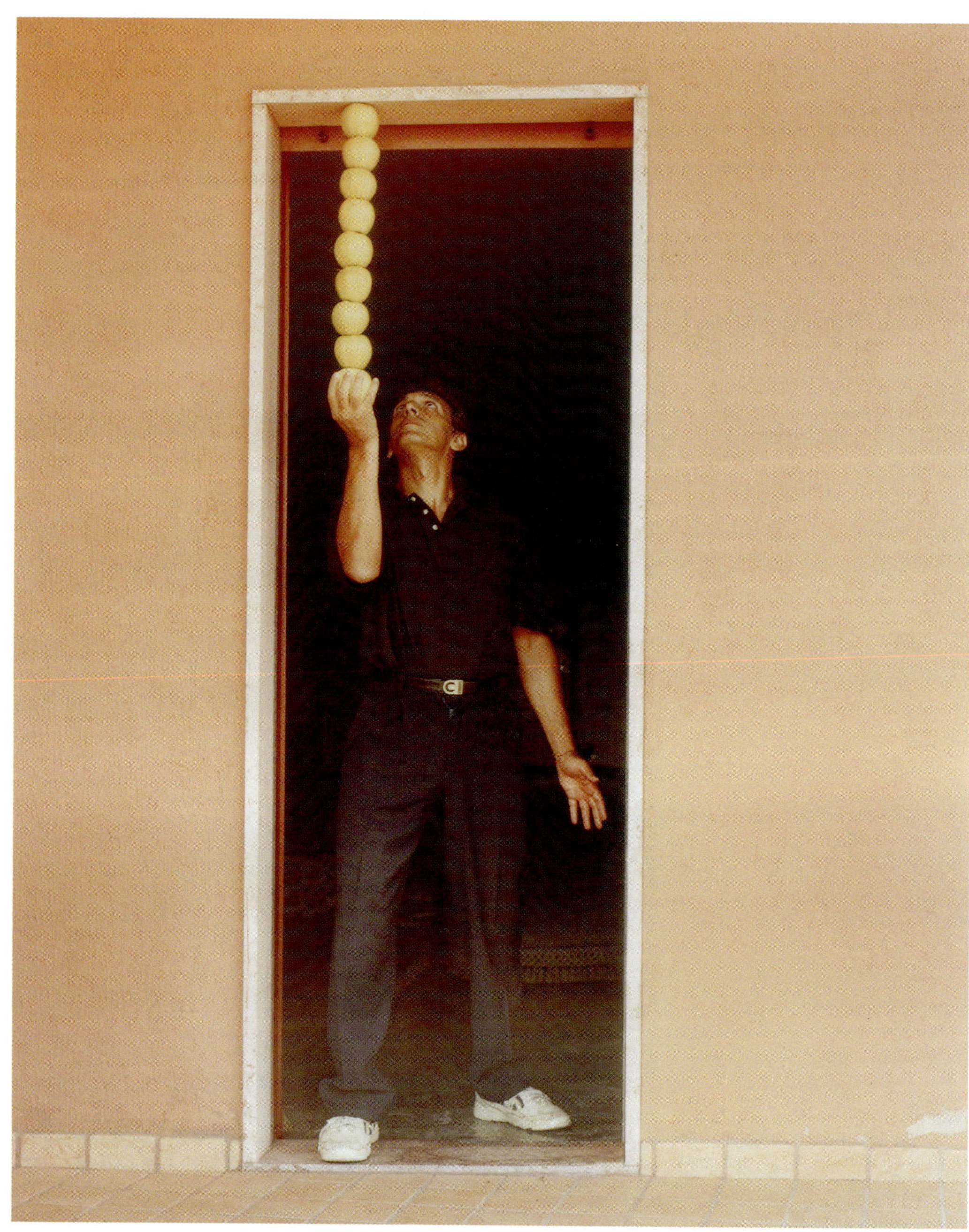

Man in the Doorway, 2006

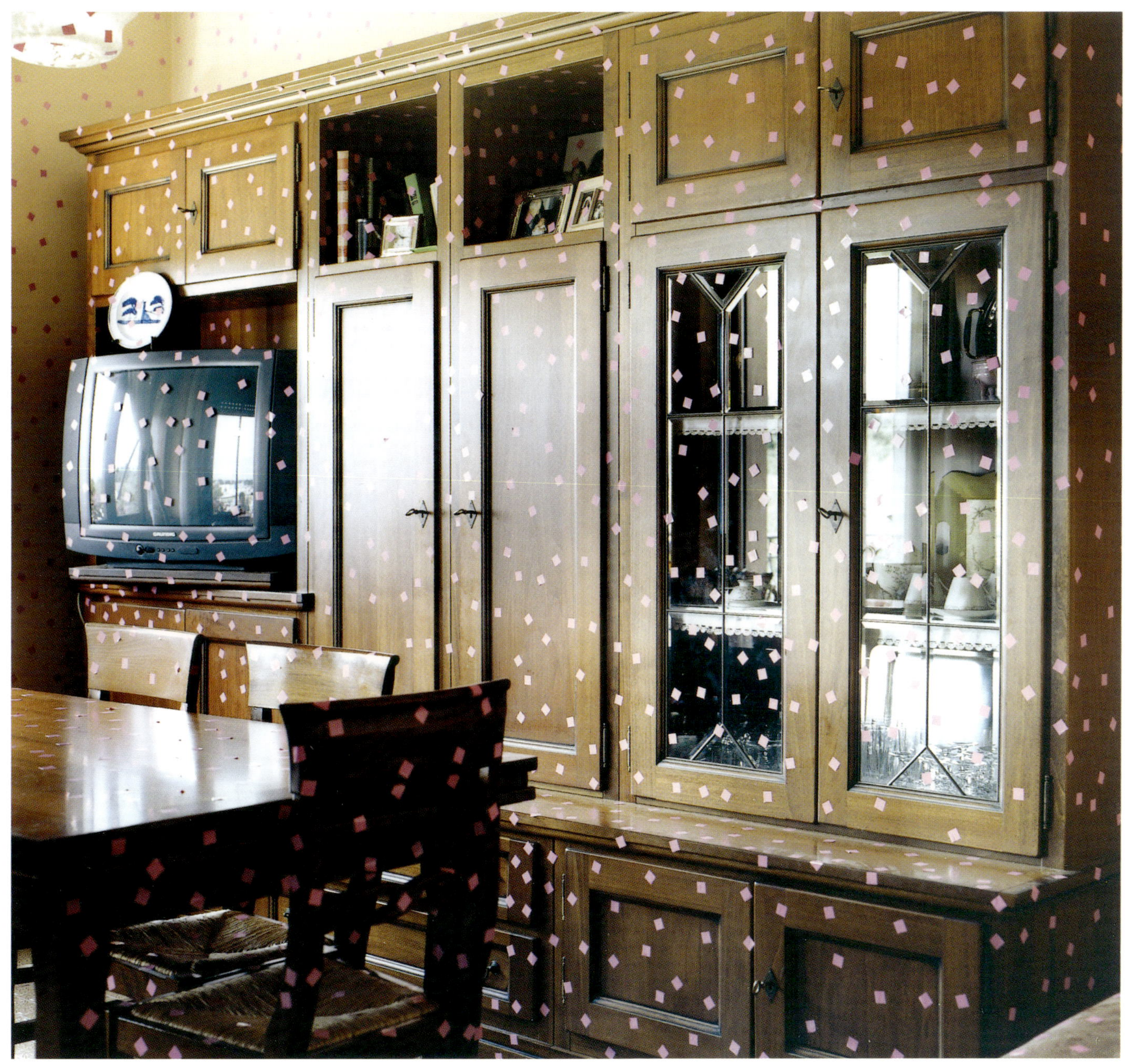

Untitled, 2006

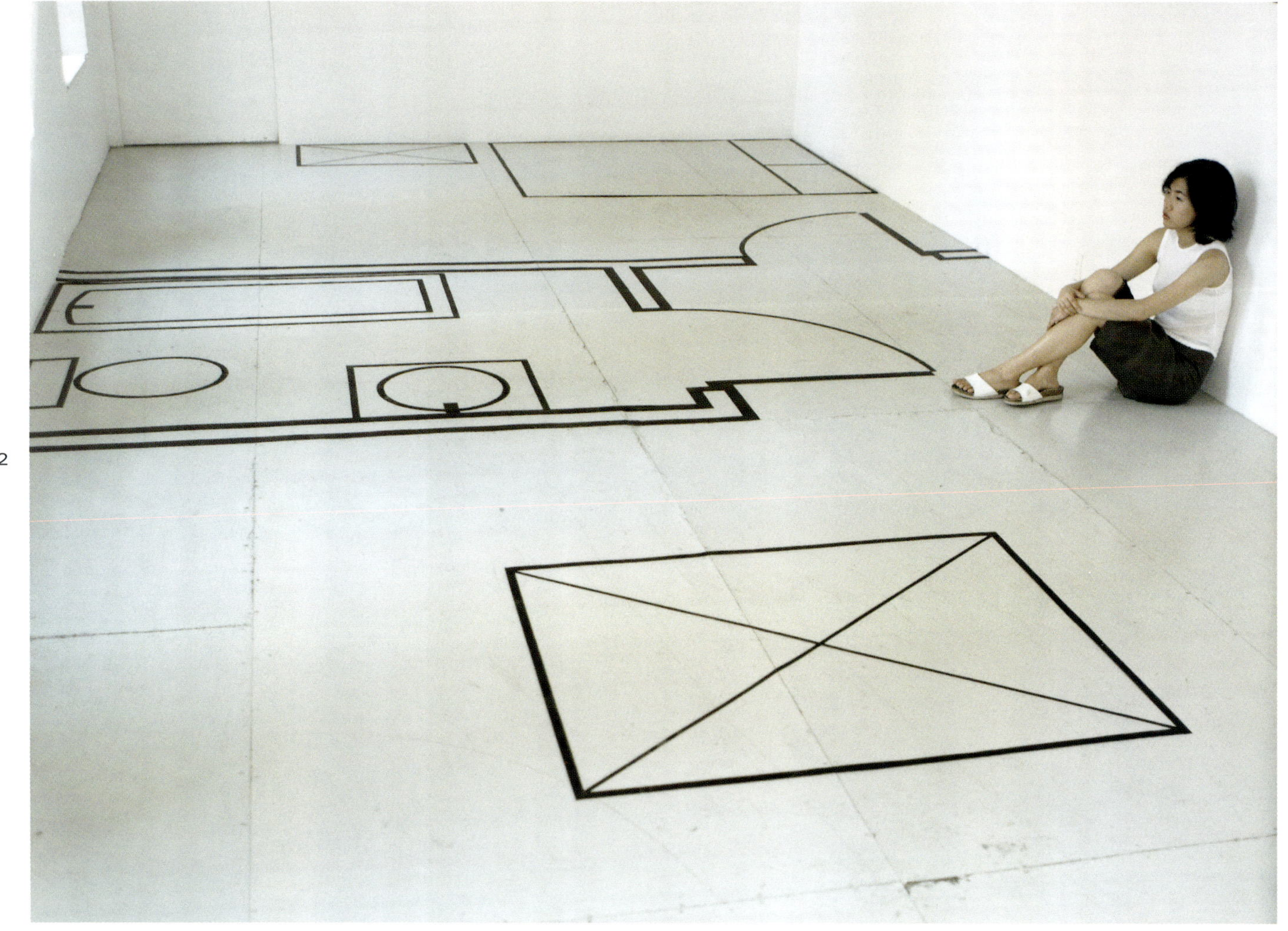

62

The Appearance and Disappearance of My Room, 2002

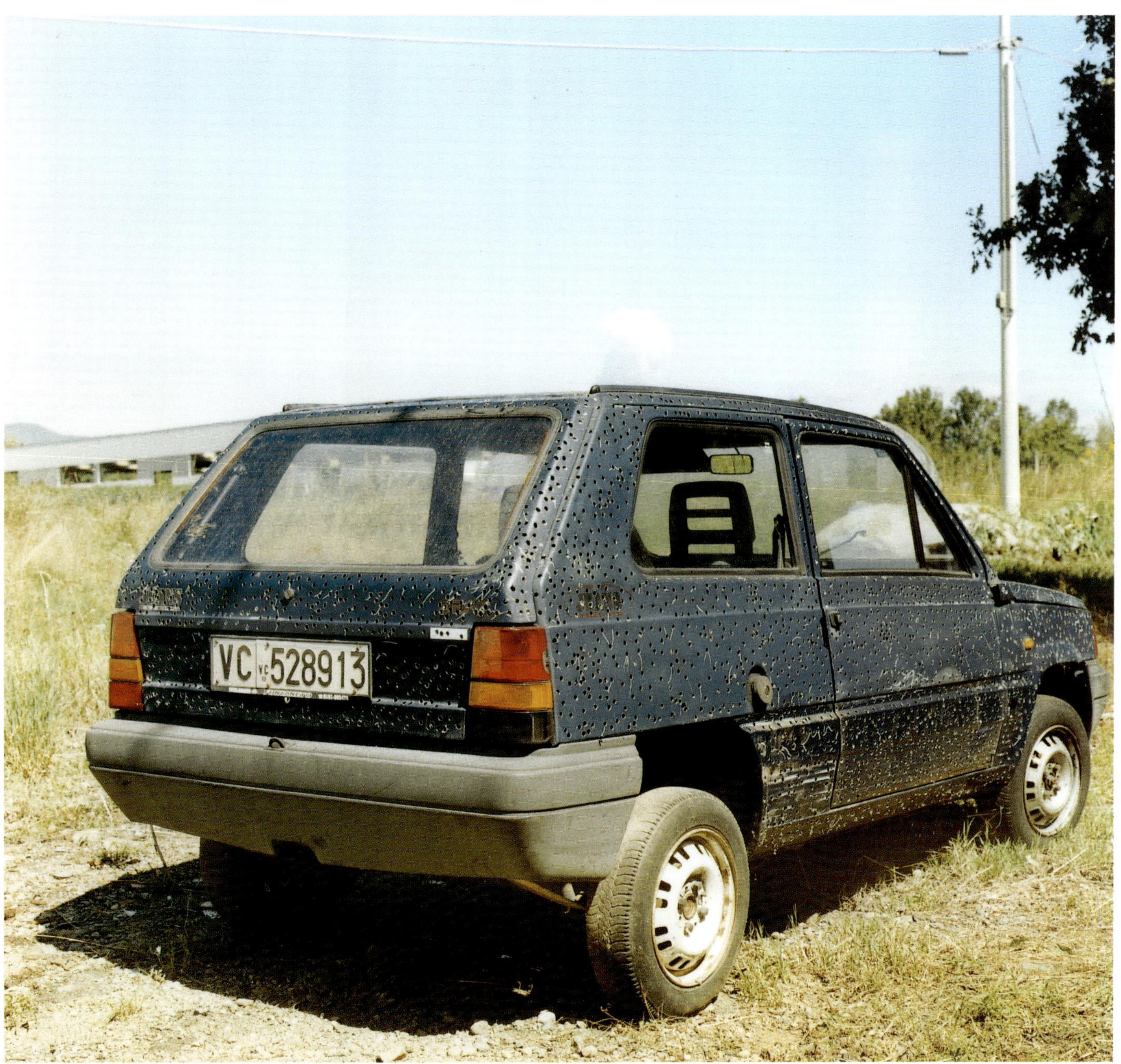

Blue Car, 2006

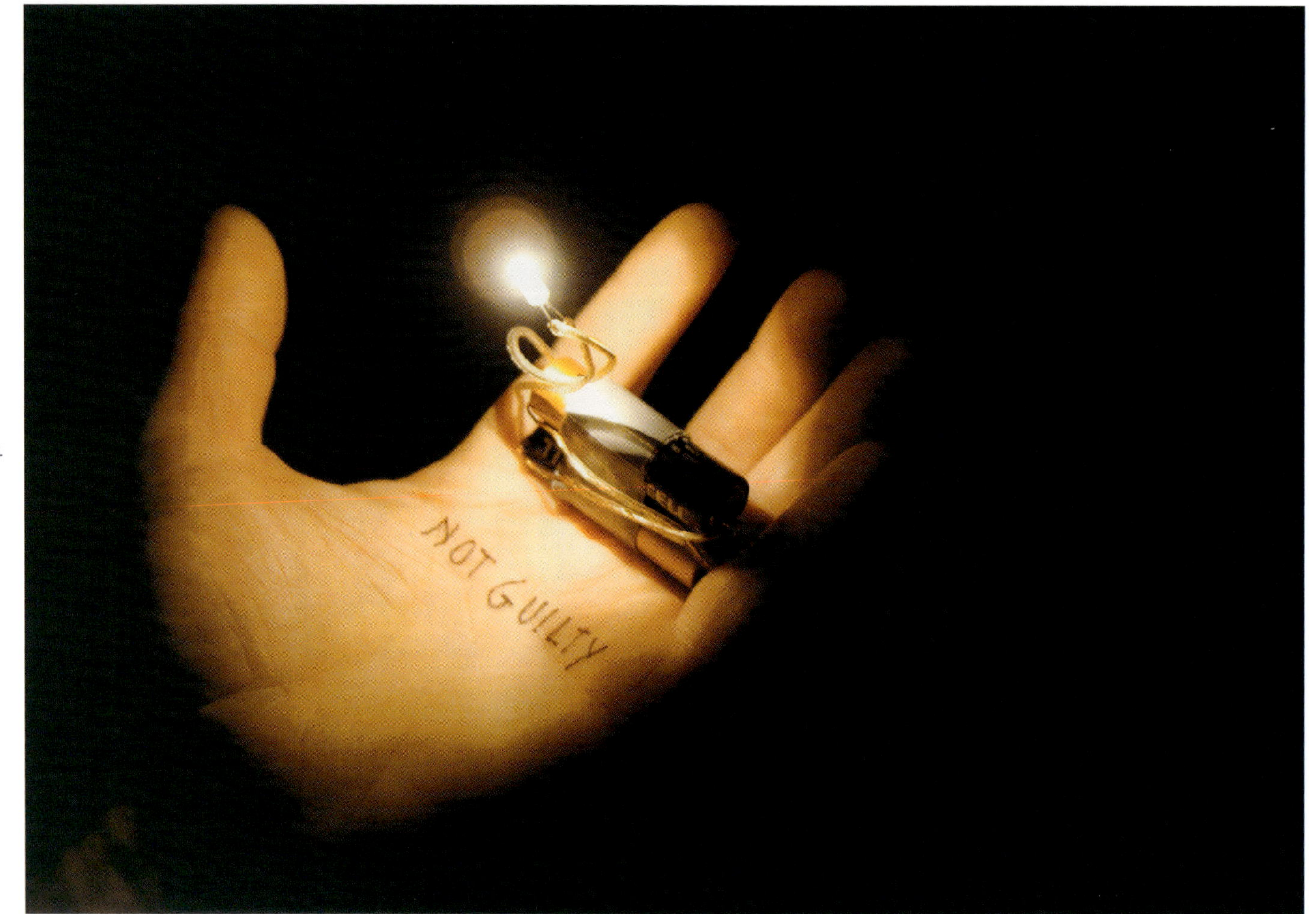

Not Guilty, 2007

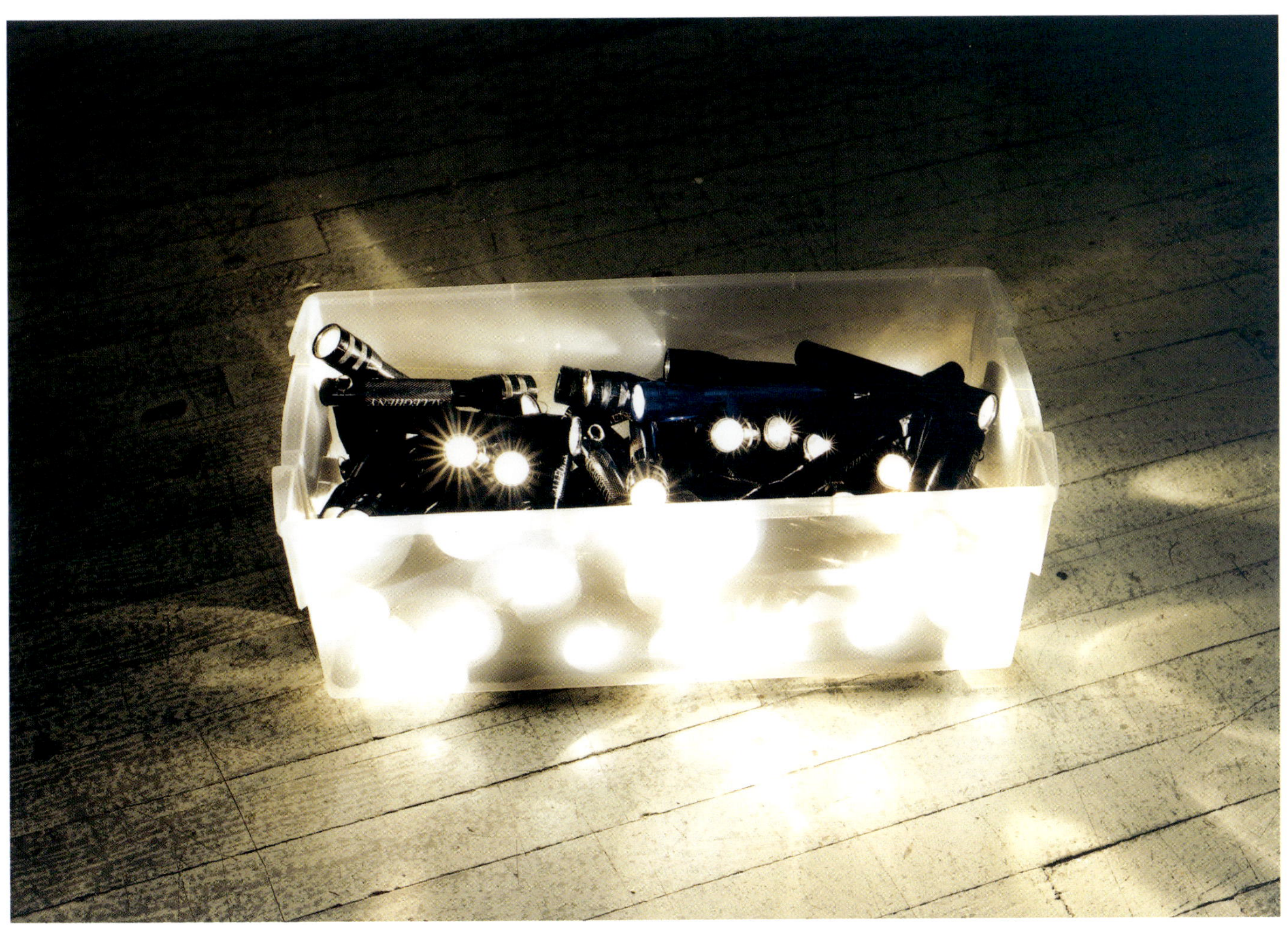

65

Torch, 2007

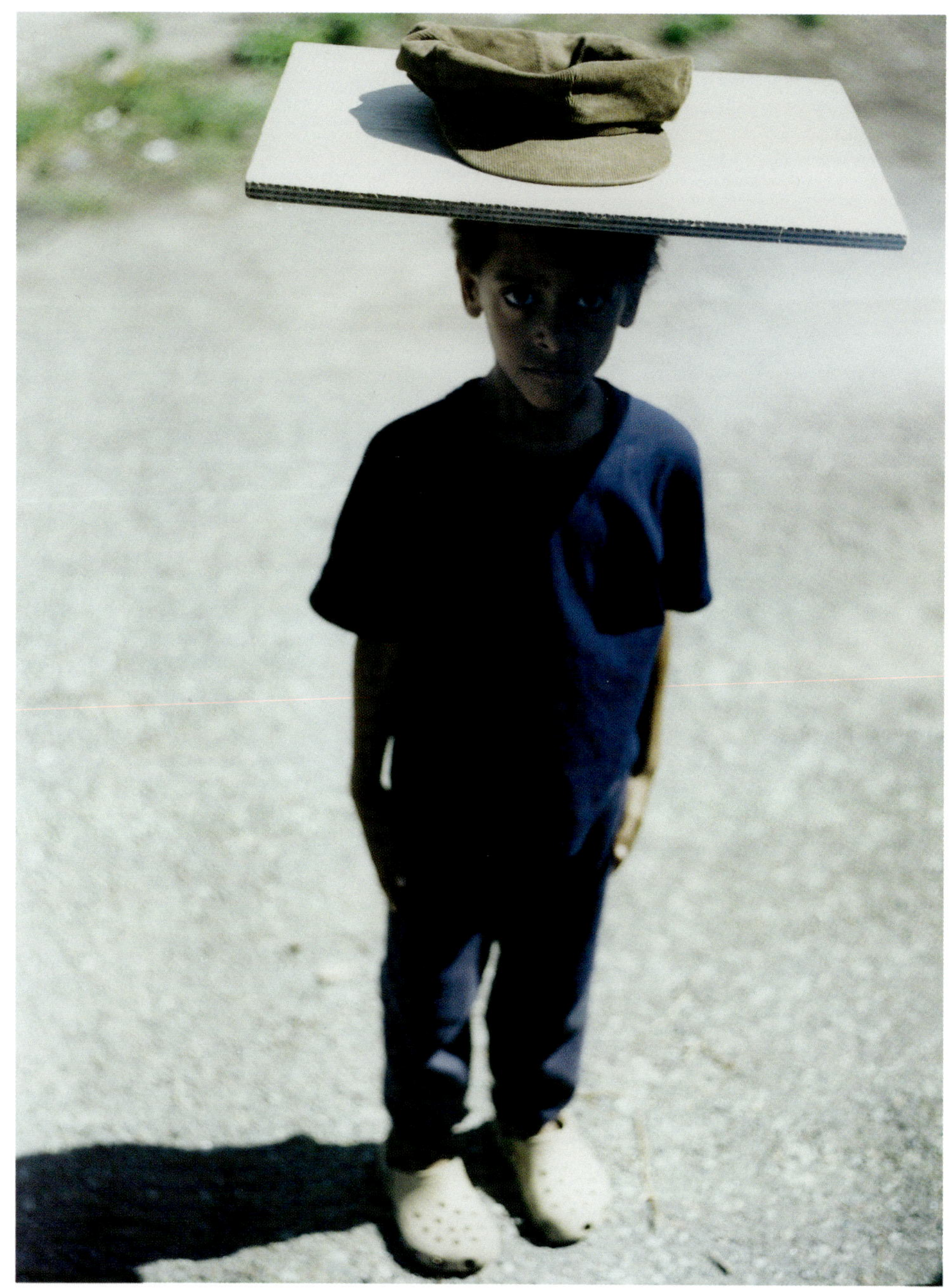

Hat, 2007

66

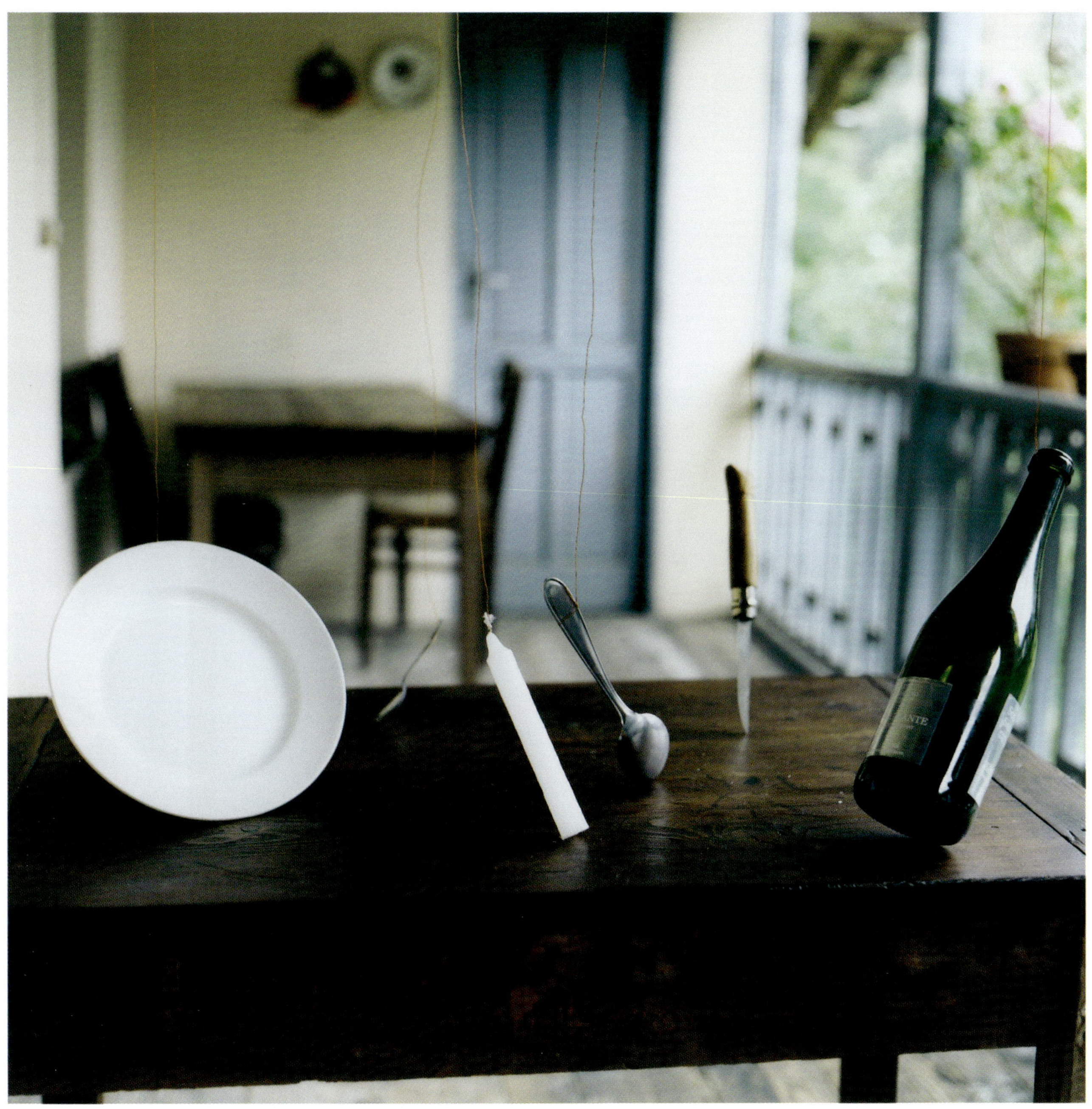

Lobbia, 2007

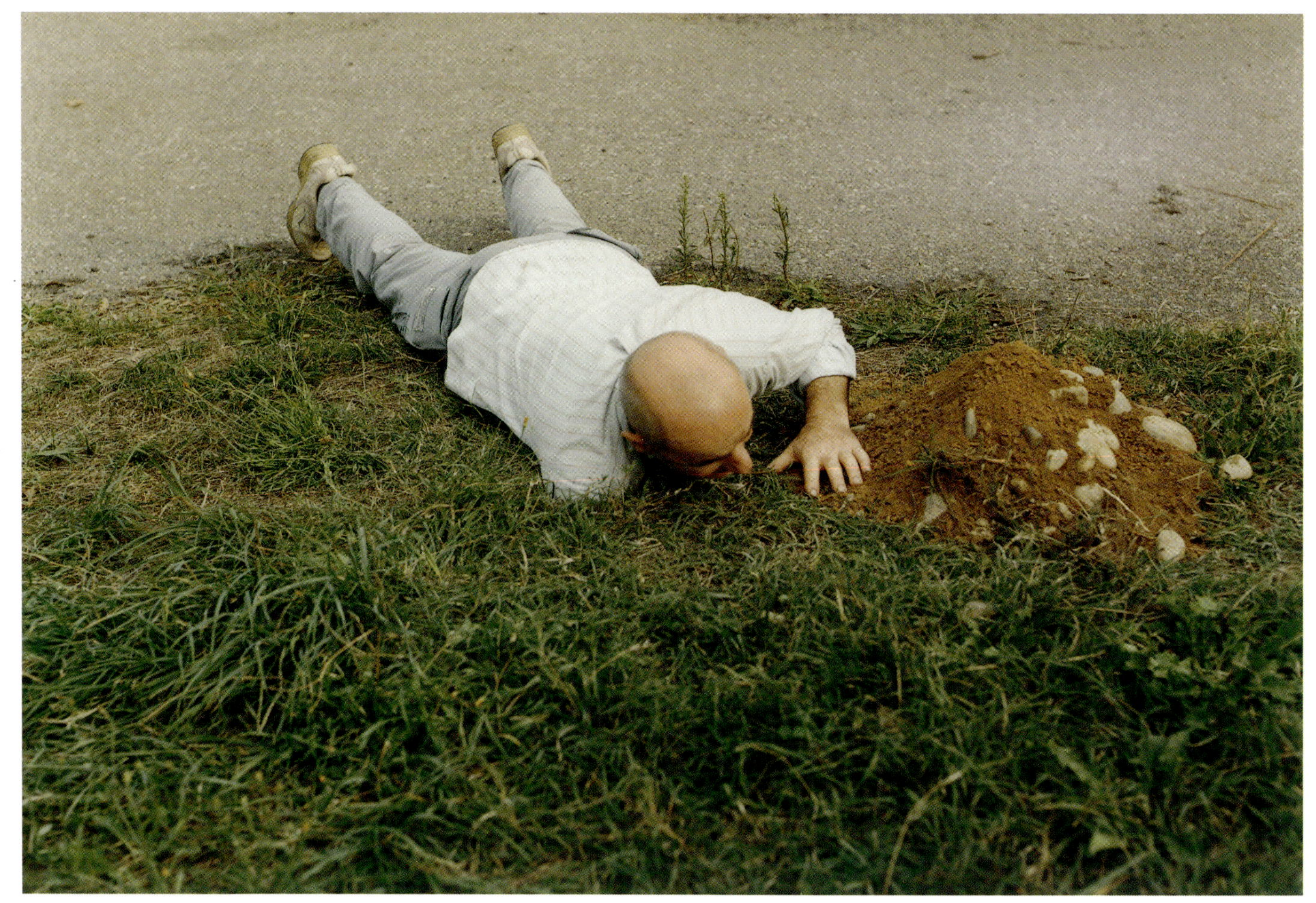

Full Tunnel, 2006

All the photographs
have been printed
40 x 50 inches in an
edition of five, and
14 x 11 inches in an
edition of seven.

Biography

Born in the Piedmont region of Italy in 1960, Carlo Ferraris currently lives and works in New York. His work has been exhibited in solo exhibitions at Greenaway Art Gallery, Adelaide, Australia; Florence Lynch Gallery, New York; Corinne Caminade, Paris; Esso Gallery, New York; C.A. OTKRbITKA Gallery, Moscow; Galleria Disegno, Mantua; and Salvatore Ala Gallery, New York, among others. Group exhibitions include: Senko Forum, Viborg, Denmark; The Shore Institute for Contemporary Arts (SICA), Long Branch, New Jersey; Bronx Center for the Arts, New York; Queens Museum, New York; VideoFest, Detroit; Galleria Piero Cavellini, Brescia; Galerie von Fellner, Krefeld; CCNOA Center for Contemporary Non-Objective Art, Brussels; Millennium Film Workshop Inc., New York; kjubh Kunstverein, Cologne; Salle D'Exposition Centre St. Charles, University de Paris I, Sorbonne, Paris; Art in General, New York; Galerie Le Faisant, Strasbourg; London Brewery, London; and White Columns, New York.

His work has been reviewed and published as follows: Wendy Walker: *Contemporary*; Christopher Chambers: *Flash Art International*; Bethany Anne Pappalardo, *tema celeste*; Joyce Korotkin: *M Magazine*; Roberta Smith: *The New York Times*; Maria Grazia Torri: *Flash Art*; Raphael Rubinstein, *Art in America*; Anthony Iannacci: *Artforum*. Other publications include *Vogue*, *Elle Decor*, *Lacanian Ink*, *Casa Vogue*, *Art Press*, *ArtNews*, *L'Architettura*, *Juliet*, and *The Art Newspaper*, among others. Carlo Ferraris is a 2004 New York Foundation for the Arts Fellow in Photography.

To find out more about Charta, and to learn
about our most recent publications, visit

www.chartaartbooks.it

Printed in November 2007
by Leva Spa, Sesto San Giovanni (Milano)
for Edizioni Charta